DIVINITY
of Women

OTHER BOOKS AND AUDIO BOOKS
BY HEATHER B. MOORE
Women of the Book of Mormon: Insights & Inspirations
Christ's Gifts to Women
Athena
Ruby's Secret

OTHER BOOKS AND AUDIO BOOKS
BY H.B. MOORE
Out of Jerusalem: Of Goodly Parents
Out of Jerusalem: A Light in the Wilderness
Out of Jerusalem: Towards the Promised Land
Out of Jerusalem: Land of Inheritance
Abinadi
Alma
Alma the Younger
Ammon
Daughters of Jared

OTHER BOOKS AND AUDIO BOOKS
BY S. KENT BROWN
Mary and Elizabeth: Noble Daughters of God
Voices from the Dust: Book of Mormon Insights

DIVINITY
of Women

Inspiration and Insights from Women of the Scriptures

HEATHER B. MOORE & S. KENT BROWN

Covenant Communications, Inc.

Published by Covenant Communications, Inc.
American Fork, Utah

Printed in China
First Printing: March 2014

20 19 18 17 16 15 14   10 9 8 7 6 5 4 3 2 1

ISBN-13: 978-1-62108-623-9

Contents

Introduction: The Divinity of Women ix

Section One: Visionary Women 1
Sarah 3
Mother of Samson 7
Rebekah...........................11
Wife of King Lamoni.....15

Section Two: Prayer and Worship 19
Women of Galilee..........21
Lydia 23
Mary................................25
Poor Widow 29
Woman with an Issue of Blood...........................31
Eve 33
Hannah 37
Abish 41

Section Three: Prophetesses....................45
Miriam 47
Deborah 51
Huldah 55
Anna................................59

Isaiah's Wife 63
Noadiah...........................65
Elisabeth.........................69
Daughters of Philip 71

Section Four: Crossing the Line 75
Jezebel 77
Rahab 81
Isabel 83
Daughter of Jared II.......85
Gomer..............................87

Section Five: Education of Ancient Women 91
Queen of Sheba 95
Queen Esther.................97
Wives of Jared and His Brother 101
Sariah 105

Conclusion: Our Divine Nature............................109

Endnotes.......................117

Introduction
The Divinity of Women

IN STUDYING THE WOMEN FOUND in scripture, we witness how those who are righteous are able to carve out their divinity and achieve their divine destinies, whereas those who do not keep the Lord's commandments suffer needlessly without the loving embrace of the Savior.

Each of us possesses divinity. We have the potential to become exalted like our Heavenly Father and His Son, Jesus Christ. We are created in His image, giving us a divine nature and destiny, which "The Family: A Proclamation to the World" explains: "All human beings—male and female—are created in the image of God. Each is a beloved spirit son or daughter of heavenly parents, and, as such, each has a divine nature and destiny."[1]

Divinity may have begun in physical form with Adam and Eve, when "God created man in his own image . . . male and female" (Genesis 1:27), but the spiritual form of divinity began before our birth, at the beginning of time, and can be refined as we grow in knowledge and works. Our first parents achieved divinity through their works on this earth; and just as Eve's divine spiritual choices led to the start of the human race, women today can carry on that divine calling our first mother accepted.

Divinity is ours for the taking. We can become exalted through Christ too. By remembering the challenges of women who precede us throughout the ages and studying how they have overcome those challenges, we are reminded that *how* we deal with our own challenges is what creates our divinity.

We have a choice in every aspect of our lives, in every challenge we face, and each choice becomes a step forward or a step back along the path of divinity. When trials come, we must remember we have a divine nature, we are lawful heirs in our Father's kingdom, and He wants to exalt us. Remembering the meaning of our divine inheritance enables us to move forward with strength in that knowledge when we face difficult times (see D&C 86:9).

Achieving our divine potential comes with responsibility, which we will review as we study the ancient women of the scriptures. Our privilege to be born in this modern world is two-fold. First, we can learn from those who have gone before us, and second, we are witnesses of "the restoration of all things spoken by the mouths of all the holy prophets since the world began" (D&C 86:10).

Therefore, our responsibility as witnesses is great. The Lord tells us, "For of him unto whom much is given much is required; and he who sins against the greater light shall receive the greater condemnation" (D&C 82:3). We have the greater knowledge; thus, we have the greater responsibility. We may rejoice in this because we also know what is at the end of life's journey: redemption and exaltation. Hope comes in the knowledge that we have the ability to reach our divine potential.

No matter our challenges and setbacks, each day we can continue to put one foot forward on the path to fulfilling our divine roles. This is paramount in rolling the Lord's plan forward as we become, in His eyes, saviors to His people: "Blessed are ye if ye continue in my goodness, a light unto the Gentiles, and through this priesthood, a savior unto my people Israel" (D&C 86:11).

Each woman has her own path to follow, one filled with joy as well as pain and sorrow. None is exempt. Our missions may vary. But we are all blessed with the opportunity to become like our Heavenly Parents.

We live in "perilous times," according to the Apostle Paul, and therefore, we must hold our divinity even closer. Many are at risk of becoming like the women Paul prophesies of in the last days: "Women laden with sins, led away with divers lusts" (2 Timothy 3:1, 6). In fact, we may know women who have taken these paths. In these perilous times, let's look to the righteous women around us and those who have gone before us to find supreme examples of the divinity of women. Let's *become* those examples, lift up those who have stumbled, and extend our love and patience. Let's learn from the women who face many tempests, and let's teach our children the things we have learned.

We are counseled by modern-day Apostles to learn from the lessons of the past.[2] Among the stories in the scriptures, we find many examples of women who are faithful followers of Christ and who have stood again and again after they've stumbled. In the stories of Miriam, Deborah, Anna, and Elisabeth, we learn how singular devotion prepares women to prophesy and to serve.

In the tumultuous examples of Queen Jezebel, Rahab, Isabel, and the daughter of King Jared II, we discover women whose lives are made impossibly difficult by poor choices and who are left without the Light of Christ to cling to in their dark days. Yet we can learn from their experiences what not to pursue in our lives.

Among those such as Sarah, the Queen of Sheba, Rebekah, and King Lamoni's wife, we can study the inspiration that comes as they open their hearts to the Spirit and follow the Lord's celestial counsel.

Divine blessings given to women are prevalent as we read about the lives of Mary, the woman with the issue of blood, Abish, Hannah, and Mother Eve. Queen Esther and Sariah become supreme examples of women who share their education and encourage additional learning in those around them.

A woman's presence here on earth is a testament that she accepts the role of a noble daughter of God. The Lord's plan includes the exaltation of His daughters, whom He cannot forget, for He has "graven [them] upon the palms of [His] hands" (Isaiah 49:16).

What a comfort and assurance to us all. No matter our challenges, through Christ, we can achieve our spiritual divinity, just as the women of old. Our value is no less in the eyes of the Lord than a queen or a prophetess is in the eyes of the world. As we remain steadfast, our faithful natures will blossom into sure knowledge and eternal reward, raising and lifting us up into the spheres of divinity itself.

We are counseled by modern-day Apostles to learn from the lessons of the past.[2] Among the stories in the scriptures, we find many examples of women who are faithful followers of Christ and who have stood again and again after they've stumbled. In the stories of Miriam, Deborah, Anna, and Elisabeth, we learn how singular devotion prepares women to prophesy and to serve.

In the tumultuous examples of Queen Jezebel, Rahab, Isabel, and the daughter of King Jared II, we discover women whose lives are made impossibly difficult by poor choices and who are left without the Light of Christ to cling to in their dark days. Yet we can learn from their experiences what not to pursue in our lives.

Among those such as Sarah, the Queen of Sheba, Rebekah, and King Lamoni's wife, we can study the inspiration that comes as they open their hearts to the Spirit and follow the Lord's celestial counsel.

Divine blessings given to women are prevalent as we read about the lives of Mary, the woman with the issue of blood, Abish, Hannah, and Mother Eve. Queen Esther and Sariah become supreme examples of women who share their education and encourage additional learning in those around them.

A woman's presence here on earth is a testament that she accepts the role of a noble daughter of God. The Lord's plan includes the exaltation of His daughters, whom He cannot forget, for He has "graven [them] upon the palms of [His] hands" (Isaiah 49:16).

What a comfort and assurance to us all. No matter our challenges, through Christ, we can achieve our spiritual divinity, just as the women of old. Our value is no less in the eyes of the Lord than a queen or a prophetess is in the eyes of the world. As we remain steadfast, our faithful natures will blossom into sure knowledge and eternal reward, raising and lifting us up into the spheres of divinity itself.

Section One
Visionary Women

WHAT A WONDERFUL GIFT IT is to receive personal revelation—an unspeakable confirmation from God to guide us along the right path to salvation. Revelation is a key component to understanding the gospel and knowing what God expects of us. It comes in many forms, including inspiration that comes as we listen during prayer, spiritual promptings, dreams, visitations, and visions. Each of us can receive personal revelation for our own benefit and for those who stand inside our stewardships.[3] Most of us won't have intense experiences or receive visions or visitations, but the personal revelations that do come to us, no matter how subtle and quiet, are a gift to cherish from the Highest.

Some of the more notable women in the scriptures who have received revelations include Sarah, wife of Abraham; Samson's mother; Rebekah; and a Lamanite queen. As we read about the revelations given to these women, our own testimonies can be strengthened, and we can come to a greater understanding of how we can receive revelation and act upon it, propelling us along our divine path.

Sarah, Wife of Abraham

Now Abraham and Sarah were old and well stricken in age; and it ceased to be with Sarah after the manner of women. (Genesis 18:11)

Not only is Sarai the wife of a prophet, but through revelation, Abram receives special instructions from the Lord for her. [4] When Sarai is ninety, the Lord changes her name to Sarah (see Genesis 17:15, 17), and Abram's name to Abraham (see v. 5). Sarah means "princess"—which might explain the reason behind her name change, since she is to conceive and bear a son, becoming "a mother of nations; [and] kings of people shall be of her" (v. 16).

Even though the Lord has promised her husband that his posterity will be vaster than the number of stars in the sky (see Genesis 15:5), Sarah falters in her own faith in the Lord's plan. She is barren for decades and believes motherhood will never come to her. At the age of seventy, it appears she's given up on the Lord's promise, and instead of continuing her wait on the Lord's timetable, she takes matters into her own hands. Sarah gives her husband the handmaiden Hagar in order to continue his posterity and fulfill the Abrahamic Covenant.[5]

However, Sarah's short-sighted view of her barrenness trial eventually leads to more challenges. We can well understand her motivation, as each of us has motivations to make things happen when we aren't willing to wait upon the Lord's timetable. She has already endured many years of feeling as though the Lord is neglecting her. Unfortunately, her solution to give another woman to her husband for the purpose of conceiving a child brings a new round of heartache in her life.

The grief Sarah endures by having to share her husband with Hagar and watching them produce a son, Ishmael, together finally ends when a long-awaited blessing comes to Sarah. She becomes pregnant with Isaac after the Lord tells her husband she will conceive. She recognizes the miracle and becomes a witness to the fulfillment of the Lord's express vision delivered to her husband. What a wonderful and comforting affirmation. Yet her challenges are far from over, and despite the gift Sarah has received, her journey to personal divinity continues.

Sarah is faced with Hagar's "mocking" (Genesis 21:9). Tensions rise to a point that Sarah asks Abraham to cast out Hagar and Ishmael so Sarah's son, Isaac, will be the undisputed heir. If Sarah does not do this, Hagar will continue to dispute Ishmael's birthright.

With Hagar departed, and now that Sarah finally has her little family gathered around her without additional parties involved, her greatest trial is about to begin. Because she has been a witness that the Lord's wisdom is greater than her own, this knowledge most likely gives her strength to endure the unspeakable loss of her son Isaac (see Genesis 22:1–2). Similarly, in our own lives, enduring one trial prepares us to meet the next.

Some artists depict Isaac as a young lad when he journeys with his father to the land of Moriah in order to participate in a burnt offering (see v. 2). Retellings of the story throughout the ages describe a boy who is surprised at his father's intentions. But biblical scholars explain that Isaac is an adult, likely in his thirties, who willingly submits to the sacrifice once he discovers its true purpose. This brings a deeper meaning to the day Sarah bids farewell to her husband and only son—Abraham knows the purpose of the journey, so it's likely Sarah knows as well and thinks she's seeing her son alive for the last time.[6]

Sarah's heart must be breaking. Her only child and son, who came after so many years of barrenness, is now leaving to become her husband's sacrifice to the Lord. This challenge tops all that she has endured so far; yet at this point, she has learned to put her whole trust in the Lord, and she humbles herself greatly and submits her will to the Lord's. We can only imagine her feelings—and prayers—as she sees Abraham and Isaac disappear from view.

Like Sarah, we can take comfort in knowing the Lord's hand is in all things, even when those things are not on an earthly timetable. We probably won't be asked to physically sacrifice our most cherished possession to the Lord, but we are asked to make sacrifices in many other areas of our lives. Sometimes we question our trials and don't regard them with an eternal perspective. We are counseled by our modern-day leaders to seek the comfort of the Holy Spirit through prayer, fasting, and scripture study.[7] And then, like Sarah, we need to turn our will over to the Lord's. But the effort is hard.

The oneness of Sarah's vision with the Lord's is not a simple journey for her; she spends many hours in doubt, fear, and frustration. Yet as she molds her will to the Lord's, she enjoys a refinement and a deeper relationship with the Lord, all part of finding her divine role.

Similar to Sarah, there will be times in our lives when we have to make great sacrifices. The Lord knows us and remembers us, and He will bless us for our sacrifices. Sarah learns the blessings that come from sacrifice on many occasions as she aligns her vision with the Lord's, and we too cannot forget that the Lord knows us on a personal level, and He will not forget us: "He forgetteth not the cry of the humble" (Psalm 9:12).

Scriptures referencing Sarah: Genesis 11:29–31; 17:15; 21:2; 23:2; Isaiah 51:2; Romans 4:19; Hebrews 11:11; 1 Peter 3:6.

Mother of Samson

For, lo, thou shalt conceive, and bear a son; and no razor shall come on his head: for the child shall be a Nazarite unto God from the womb: and he shall begin to deliver Israel out of the hand of the Philistines.
(Judges 13:5)

ANGELS' VISITS ARE RARE. BUT an angel comes to the mother of Samson twice, indicating that the Lord sees her for who she really is, and He blesses her with added instruction. In contrast, in the eyes of her family and acquaintances, her inability to have children opens her to a "reproach among men [and women]" in her hillside village (Luke 1:25). In this era, barrenness is considered a curse from the Lord as a result of the woman's sin since one of the primary duties of a wife is to produce an heir for her husband.

We, of course, know barrenness is not a curse but a physical or medical condition, like many other challenges women or men may face. Women today who face similar challenges of infertility may feel the Lord has neglected them as others around them seem to bear children with no difficulty. Yet, it is apparent from the story of Samson's mother that she is far from neglected. With or without a child, the Lord knows her and enables her ultimate divine mission on His own timetable.[8]

Adding to the remarkable nature of Samson's mother's story of endurance is the knowledge that her society is mired deep in apostasy: "The children of Israel did evil again in the sight of the Lord; and the Lord delivered them into the hand of the Philistines forty years" (Judges 13:1). At the end of these forty years, "the angel of the Lord appeared unto the woman" (v. 3). Remarkably, living in a time of such repressive turmoil, she somehow manages to stay true to her beliefs, just as many of us do today, despite less-than-ideal circumstances. Our rewards likely won't include an angelic visit, but we can be sure our faithfulness and endurance is noticed on high.

In Samson's mother's case, the angel brings stunning news: "Thou shalt conceive, and bear a son" (v. 3). With this announcement, of course, the Lord obliges Himself to perform a miracle for a childless woman, just as He does for Sarah and Rachel, for Hannah and Elisabeth, placing Samson's mother in very select company. But there is more.

Her child of promise will have "no razor . . . come on his head" (Judges 13:5; 16:17), and she is to avoid "any thing that cometh of the vine" (Judges 13:14); her diet must exclude "any unclean thing" (v. 4, 14). Her willingness to obey these dietary restrictions in response to her visions forms an essential supporting structure for her son's success as a deliverer of his people. To get this far, she has developed her divine nature to the point that the Lord can trust her. Yet to continue in her growth, the Lord gives her more responsibility and strictures. Does she fulfill her part in supporting her son? Yes—including counseling him on marital choices. It becomes clear that she wants her son to marry someone who stands within the covenant of their people (see Judges 14:2–3).

This woman, barren and otherwise unknown, becomes the Lord's choice to raise a special son who will deliver her people from bondage. She is willing to take whatever measures necessary to support her son and seems to easily and graciously abide by the dietary limitations the Lord places on her, indicating her firmly obedient character. She involves herself as a guide to her son, even into his adult years.[9]

It's important to know that her journey toward purification isn't secured with the angel's appearances to her. She cannot rest on any perceived laurels that the angel's visits bring. She is asked to further purify herself and to continue in a life of obedience and worship as she raises her son. We know very well that our challenges today are not few and that they continue, no matter the height of the mountains we have already climbed. As with Samson's mother, even though she is worthy to have an angel visit her, she is still asked to be better, to be obedient, and to endure. Likewise, the Lord asks us to continually press forward and upward until we reach the pinnacle upon which He wishes us to stand.

Scriptures referencing Samson's mother:
Judges 13:2–24; 14:1–9, 16; 16:17.

Rebekah

And Isaac brought her into his mother Sarah's tent, and took Rebekah, and she became his wife; and he loved her. (Genesis 24:67)

IF A MODERN NEWS REPORTER were to meet Rebekah, wife of Isaac, and ask about the most joyous moments in her life, it would not be surprising if she said one of her happiest moments came on the day she learned she would have children (see Genesis 25:20–21). We can only imagine her joy. But Rebekah's life is not easy with or without children. That moment, though, when she senses the Lord's help in bringing children to her, stands as the guiding star of her life.

One important extension of that experience provides Rebekah with the strength to face whatever trial she is dealt when she is entrusted with the news about the relationship between her unborn twin boys, Esau and Jacob. Significantly, she feels discomfort during her pregnancy that drives her to the Lord, indicating that the discomfort is heaven-sent because the Lord wants to reveal to her this secret (see v. 22): "Two nations are in thy womb," the Lord says about her pregnancy, "and the one people shall be stronger than the other people; and the elder shall serve the younger" (v. 23). Most women would be elated to be told they are having twins, but Rebekah is told even before they are born that her sons' relationship will not be a peaceful one. This divine communiqué becomes an all-important additional blessing in her life and guides her every step in raising her sons.

As an example, she frets when Esau decides to marry outside the covenant because "Esau . . . took to wife Judith the daughter of Beeri the Hittite, and Bashemath the daughter of Elon the Hittite: Which were a grief of mind unto . . . Rebekah" (Genesis 26:34–35). How much of a concern are these brides to Rebekah? Later we hear her complaining to Isaac: "I am weary . . . because of the daughters of Heth [Hittites]." Her fear rises to a higher pitch because the choices for her son Jacob are limited among their neighbors: "If Jacob take a wife of the daughters of Heth, such as these [their daughters-in-law] which are of the daughters of the land, what good shall my life do me?" (Genesis 27:46).

This is a question many across the ages ask—if my child makes this choice or that choice, what good am I? We can take comfort as Rebekah takes comfort in how her earlier experiences have taught her that the Lord's ways are to be trusted. When we seek the Lord in faithfulness, we can secure His help.

The result of Rebekah's worry comes about when she coaches Jacob to pose as Esau so he will receive the chief blessing—the birthright Esau has already given up (see Genesis 25:29–34; 27:1–30). She knows the birthright is an important possession and that one cannot keep it with missteps in marriage. Therefore, when Esau breathes out threats against Jacob after he acquires the birthright, Rebekah and Isaac send Jacob back to her family in Haran, far away from the land of Canaan, where he will have a chance to marry in the covenant. Rebekah's strategy works because in the house of Laban, Rebekah's brother, Jacob finds Leah and Rachel (see Genesis 27:41–28:5; 29:1–30). All of this occurs because of the guiding revelation that comes to Rebekah while she is still expecting her twins.[10]

Above all, Rebekah remains faithful, regularly relying on the guidance of the Lord throughout her life because of her experiences during pregnancy wherein she learns of the Lord's interest in her. Although Rebekah's challenges change as her children mature, she forges on because she knows the Lord knows and cares for her and her family members. In addition to the strong testimony and assurance she receives through revelation from the Lord, Rebekah continues in faithfulness and endurance.

Just as the Lord knows Rebekah, He knows the agony and worry mothers feel for their children now. Just like He understands Rebekah, the Lord understands the constant anxiety women have today over their decisions, and He will lead us if we trust in Him. The Lord is waiting for us to seek Him so He can fulfill His promises to us.

Scriptures referencing Rebekah: Genesis 24; 25:19–28; 26:6–12, 34–35; 27:1–29; 27:41–28:7.

Wife of King Lamoni

Now the queen having heard of the fame of Ammon, therefore she sent
and desired that he should come in unto her. (Alma 19:2)

A HEAVENLY VISION COMES TO a Lamanite queen, similar to the vision
of her husband, King Lamoni, when Ammon testifies of the Savior.
Before the event of the queen's vision, she enacts two measures of faith
when she's told her husband is dead: first, she puts off burying her
husband, and second, she consults with the Nephite Ammon. These are
significant since they demonstrate that the queen is already acting on
her faith, and only after these valiant efforts does the vision come.

The scriptures teach us that a testimony or confirmation comes
only "after the trial of [our] faith" (Ether 12:6). Praying, fasting, and
keeping our temple covenants are all acts of faith when we are seeking
answers to important questions. Like the Lamanite queen, we may have
to take these steps before the answers come.

In the queen's Lamanite kingdom, Ammon is a former enemy and
now a servant (see Alma 19:2–5). Why should she listen to a Nephite,
let alone a servant? Especially over her trusted advisors? We know the
answer—the Spirit has been whispering to her and negating any other
preconceived reaction a Lamanite queen should have. And the answers
to her prayers may surprise her, but she has been prepared. At times the
Lord brings us to our knees in grief and sorrow in order for us to be
receptive to His message.

The grieving queen seems to be at a point of such deep humility that
she's ready to listen to a higher voice, even though she doesn't completely
understand who He is. The promptings of the Spirit give her the courage
to act in a manner that may not be consistent with her upbringing.

These bits of faith enacted on the queen's part are not insignificant and act as a precursor to a greater event to come—an event that touches her soul and changes the religious fiber of her kingdom. Up until Ammon teaches the king and his court, the Lamanite queen has been worshiping idols, such as the jaguar god, so the queen's vision becomes a three-sixty turnaround event.[11]

Despite her previous religious beliefs, her convictions change dramatically when she becomes a witness to Ammon's teachings through her personal vision from the Lord.

The queen's change of heart comes when she is willing ask a Nephite for advice. She has to tread carefully because, while her husband is temporarily comatose, she is the only functioning ruler of the kingdom. Not only is her husband's fate at stake but also her position and her children's royal future in the kingdom.

Asking for help can be difficult, even when prompted or when taking a step in faith in order to do it. Despite the queen's inspired decision to seek Ammon's counsel, she has valid concerns and possibly doubts in doing so. What if the king is truly dead and the people hold Ammon responsible? Will they turn on the queen because she seeks a Nephite's advice? The seed of faith takes firm root when she pushes her worries aside and asks Ammon for his opinion. Her faith is rewarded when Ammon tells her that, yes, Lamoni is alive and then asks her, "Believest thou this?" (Alma 19:9).

Her reply is bold yet humble: "I have had no witness save thy word, and the word of our servants; nevertheless I believe that it shall be according as thou hast said" (v. 9).

Ammon's answer is remarkable, especially when we consider that he is the son of King Mosiah. He's also a contemporary of Alma the Elder and Alma the Younger and has done a great deal of missionary work throughout the land of Zarahemla: "Blessed art thou because of thy exceeding faith; I say unto thee, woman, *there has not been such great faith among all the people of the Nephites*" (v. 10, emphasis added).

Here we meet a Lamanite woman, a queen no less, who is now counted among one of the most faithful of her generation. This great faith of a Lamanite queen is further attested to when King Lamoni calls her "blessed" after he arises the next day (v. 12). She becomes a remarkable example of how we can follow a single prompting of the Spirit and how that consequence can bless many others.

As soon as Lamoni testifies of the Redeemer and falls to the ground again, the queen falls as well, overcome by the power of God, and experiences her own marvelous vision (see vv. 13–15). The queen no longer operates on faith alone but now on divine knowledge.

When the queen's servant Abish witnesses the miraculous events, she hurries out of the palace to inform the citizens and returns with her countrymen in tow, but their reaction is one of fear. Abish touches the queen's hand, and the queen awakens and says, "O blessed Jesus, who has saved me from an awful hell! O blessed God, have mercy on this people!" (v. 29). We don't know exactly what the queen sees in her vision besides her own salvation; regardless, she is filled with joy and testifies to her people, "speaking many words which were not understood" (v. 30).

The queen's vision precipitates a major transformation, taking her from an idol-worshiping queen to a woman with faith in the true Lord. It seems that in a short time, she has been saved from her previous sins, yet we must remember she has an open heart and is ready to accept the Lord's message. This complete change can be compared to modern-day converts to the Church whose lives undergo drastic changes in order for them to be baptized. For those of us raised in the Church, we still experience a change of heart when we pray to gain our own testimony or are faced with the need to repent. If our hearts are open, as the queen's was, our lives can be transformed.

Although we may not experience the sort of vision the queen sees, if we are willing to step forward in faith, our own vision will come.

Scriptures referencing the wife of King Lamoni:
Alma 19:2–5, 6–13, 17, 29–30.

Section Two
Prayer and Worship

From the earliest records of divine power, prayer has been part of a woman's worship practice. For example, Rachel prays to have children, and "God remembered Rachel, and God hearkened to her, and opened her womb" (Genesis 30:22). Leah prays fervently as well, as implied by the verse "God hearkened unto Leah" (v. 17).

A prayer might also be considered a pondering of the heart. When Mary, mother of Jesus, is visited by heaven-sent shepherds, we are told, "Mary kept all these [unexpected] things, and pondered them in her heart" (Luke 2:19). In the book of Samuel, Hannah is recorded as praying more than once, the first time asking for a child, the second time thanking the Lord for granting her a child (see 1 Samuel 1:9–14; 2:1–10). Other women in history, such as Judith, from the Apocrypha, fast and pray.[12]

Studying about faithful women who use prayer as a device to fulfill their divine roles as women, daughters, wives, and mothers enables each of us to take courage in their examples. We see their challenges and the manner in which they lived, and we can enjoy the comforting knowledge that the Lord provides us with a sure communication with heaven.

Women of Galilee

*There were also women looking on afar off: among whom was Mary
Magdalene, and Mary the mother of James the less and of Joses,
and Salome; (Who also, when he was in Galilee, followed him, and
ministered unto him;) and many other women which came up with him
unto Jerusalem.* (Mark 15:40–41)

FROM THE STORIES ABOUT THE Savior emerge a distinct group of
faithful women. All come from Galilee, and all are attracted early
on to Christ's message. All follow Him to Jerusalem and become first-
rank witnesses of His Resurrection because they both hear and see the
divine messengers who announce it and later see Christ too. All of these
women bear their first testimonies to the remaining eleven Apostles.
Although their words are treated "as idle tales" (Luke 24:11), the
subsequent events of that matchless day of Jesus's Resurrection prove
they are true witnesses.

Besides Jesus's mother, three notable women are recipients of Jesus's
miraculous powers, having "been healed of evil spirits and infirmities"
(Luke 8:2). The best known is Mary Magdalene, the Savior's friend
who hails from the town of Magdala, a shoreline settlement almost
five miles southwest across the Sea of Galilee from Capernaum. On
a memorable occasion, Jesus casts "seven devils" out of her. In time,
she becomes one of only three persons to whom the resurrected Lord
appears individually.[13]

Joanna, whose husband is Chuza, "Herod's steward" (v. 3), enjoys high
status in her community because of her husband's important position.

Yet, like many modern women, her heart and mind are susceptible to spiritual stimuli, and she welcomes Jesus's message, as well as His healing powers. Part of her worship of Him is that she "ministered unto him of [her] substance," assisting financially and materially in His work (v. 3). Moreover, she faithfully follows the Savior during His ministry, traveling with others all the way to Jerusalem, where, after coming to His tomb early that Sunday morning, she hears and sees the two angels who announce the Resurrection (see Luke 24:10). Furthermore, she is certainly among those who gather that evening and unexpectedly, then joyously receive a visit from the risen Jesus. In this place, Jesus instructs them through much of the night before departing from them on the road to Bethany in the early morning (see vv. 33, 36–51).

Of Susanna and "Mary the mother of James, and other women who were with them" (Luke 24:10; 8:3), we are told little. But like Mary Magdalene and Joanna, it's likely they experience the full blessing of associating with Jesus and the other disciples, especially the Twelve (see Luke 8:1). From early in Christ's ministry until that day of days on Resurrection Sunday, the women carry the message of the two angels and then spend the night listening to the resurrected Savior's voice as He instructs them, opening "their understanding, that they might understand the scriptures" (Luke 24:45). Devoted? Yes. And worshipful? On balance, this evident willingness to assist in any way they can points to something like an ancient Relief Society.[14]

In this sense, these women play an integral role in furthering the Savior's mission. It goes without saying that this is the case in our modern-day communities: charity is the resounding message of the Savior's ministry, and our Relief Society embodies and acts on this ancient virtue. When worldly avenues fail in approaching and solving life's challenges, the Savior's most powerful message can be the one thing that cuts to the heart and heals—we must have charity, the pure love of Christ.

Scriptures referencing the Galilean women: Matthew 27:55–56, 61; 28:1–10; Mark 15:40–41, 47; 16:1–11; Luke 8:2–3; 23:49, 55–56; 24:1–10, 22–24; John 19:25–27; 20:1–2, 11–18; Acts 1:14.

Lydia, "A Seller of Purple"

*And a certain woman named Lydia, a seller of purple, of the city of
Thyatira, which worshipped God, heard us: whose heart the Lord opened,
that she attended unto the things which were spoken of Paul.*
(Acts 16:14)

WHO WOULD KNOW FROM SITTING on the peaceful bank of the
Gangites River that Philippi is the site of two major battles for
control of the Roman Empire less than a century before Christ's time?
Just outside of town, next to the stream, the Apostle Paul and his friend
Luke and other traveling companions meet "a certain woman named
Lydia, a seller of purple," and other Jewish "women which resorted
thither" (Acts 16:13). The Apostle Paul conducts a worship service here
because no synagogue stands in the town and there is no *minyan*—a
group of at least ten Jewish men needed for a regular service.

Paul's impromptu message in that tranquil, reverent setting touches
Lydia in particular, "whose heart the Lord opened." Following the
service, "she was baptized," becoming the first convert on European
soil. Members of her household are also baptized. Her testimony
and her commitment are so strong that "she besought" Paul and his
associates to "come into [her] house, and abide there" (vv. 14–15; see
also Philippians 4:3).

The tranquility of this Greek town does not last long. Paul and Silas,
one of Paul's companions, are forced to leave. But before Paul and Silas
depart, they return to Lydia's home, which she has opened for church
meetings, and spend time with her and "the brethren" who have been
influenced by her missionary spirit to accept baptism (Acts 16:40). Thus,

Lydia becomes one of the anchors in the growing branch of the Church in Philippi, sharing the true gospel, and offering help and support to others from her home.[15]

Lydia is like many of us as we try to set an example for others to follow. Whether it is attending church week after week, serving in an inconspicuous calling, or living as the only active or baptized member of the Church in our family or community, through our unfailing worship, we can unknowingly inspire someone else to take a step closer to the waters of baptism. The ripple effect of the gospel and Lydia's devotion to it is a tangible thing. Most of us have had experiences when a testimony over the pulpit, a small act of thoughtfulness, or a greeting in a church hallway has left an impression on our hearts.

Just as one person's example and testimony can touch us, if we are ready to worship and open our hearts toward others, like Lydia, whether it's offering the comfort of our home to another or something else, our own example and testimony can be equally important in another's life. As we continue on our divine path, prayerfully facing the obstacles before us with the Spirit as our guide, our resulting examples will leave an indelible footprint leading into eternity.

Scriptures referencing Lydia: Acts 16:12–15, 40; Philippians 4:3.

Mary, Mother of Jesus

And the angel said unto her, Fear not, Mary: for thou hast found favour with God. (Luke 1:30)

WORSHIPFUL OCCASIONS AND SACRED EVENTS are not only important to Mary, but they are also like the air she breathes. The fact that her son Jesus attends synagogue services each Sabbath, "as his custom was" (Luke 4:16), is testimony to her own righteous routines and their enduring influence on Jesus. Three examples paint the picture.

First, when her newborn Son is forty days old, she and Joseph take Him to the temple to offer the required sacrifices for her cleansing after childbirth and to pay the five-shekel redemption fee. At the time, they are residing in Bethlehem, a five-mile trek from Jerusalem, ten miles round trip. Even though they are rather poor, as becomes clear from the offering of the two birds (see Luke 2:24; Leviticus 12:6–8), Mary and her husband make the effort to come to the temple. They enter the Court of the Women to pay the five shekels and, from there, witness the priest offering the two birds on the sacrificial altar.

The cost of a proper offering—a lamb—is more than Mary and Joseph can afford. But Mary knows spending money on an offering is the right thing to do, even if she can ill afford it, so she elects the less expensive choice of offerings and purchases two birds.

In the Court of the Women, Mary can see through the Nicanor Gate into the Court of the Priests, where sits the huge altar of sacrifice, on which two birds are offered up on her behalf. This is as close as she will ever come to the temple's sanctuary. Even so, she obviously presents herself in a spirit of obedience and worship.

Second, when Mary's Son is twelve years old, she and Joseph bring Him to the temple for the Passover (see Luke 2:41–42). This act bears witness to Mary's inner desire to go to the main house of worship, particularly at this point in her Son's life. For years, she has been excused from attending the major festivals because she has been bearing children, but she takes time from her other family responsibilities because she feels a deep need to accompany her first Son to the temple to help introduce Him to its sacred character. And we know she has other children she is leaving behind to worship with Jesus because they are noted in scripture: "Is not this the carpenter's son? . . . and his brethren, James, and Joses, and Simon, and Judas? And his sisters, are they not all with us?" (Matthew 13:55–56; also Mark 6:3). Jesus is Mary's "firstborn son," and her children with Joseph come later (Matthew 1:25).

In this manner, she is setting aside the daily chores and duties she certainly faces with a houseful of children and is focusing on an important event with her eldest Son. Spiritual nourishment and religious observance takes precedence in her life, and rightly so. Similarly, each of us has opportunities to weigh out the same events. A woman's work is seemingly never-ending, yet taking the time to properly nourish her divine self will enrich her life and those who depend on her.

Third, Mary is a very prominent participant in one of the most important meetings of disciples following her Son's Resurrection. After the death of Judas Iscariot and after the risen Savior trains the eleven Apostles for forty days (see Acts 1:3), "about an hundred and twenty" followers gather "with one accord in prayer and supplication" to witness the choosing of the man who is to succeed Judas as a member of the Twelve. Luke particularly notes the presence of "Mary the mother of Jesus" among the congregated disciples (vv. 14–15). For her and for the other followers of her Son, it is important that she be present on this momentous, sacred occasion when the new Apostle is chosen.[16] Plainly, she does not sever her inner link to the work of her Son at His death but remains connected to the ongoing efforts of His closest followers to establish an institution of worship and prayer.

Scriptures referencing Mary: Matthew 1:16, 18–25; 2:11–15, 19–23; 12:46–50; 13:55; Mark 3:31–35; 6:3; Luke 1:26–56; 2:4–52; 8:19–21; John 2:1–5, 12; 6:42; 19:25–27; Acts 1:14; 1 Nephi 11:13–21; Mosiah 3:8; Alma 7:10.

The Poor Widow at the Temple

And there came a certain poor widow, and she threw in two mites,
which make a farthing. (Mark 12:42)

ON TUESDAY OR WEDNESDAY OF the last week of Jesus's life, He observes a poor widow walking into the Court of the Women, where thirteen chests lie open to receive donations from worshipers. He points her out to His disciples, drawing attention to what she is about to do. From where the disciples are standing and sitting, the massive yet elegant sanctuary rises far above their heads, faceted with resplendent white marble and appointed with gold leaf. The stunning opulence of this main structure forms a gripping contrast to the woman dressed in worn clothing, carrying two small copper coins.

It is the worn clothing that must identify her to the Savior. To the observant person, she will stand out from the crowd, and Christ possesses a practiced and merciful eye that looks out for "the poor, the maimed, the lame, the blind" (Luke 14:13, 21). Much hides behind her shabby exterior, such as the deep devotion that drives her to the temple on an early spring day to offer a gift that will help other poor people. After all, it is the Passover season, and many, like her, take occasion to come to the temple to make their offerings.

As Jesus watches others who offer their gifts, His words frame His point about this poor woman: "All these have of their abundance cast in unto the offerings of God: but she of her penury hath cast in all that she had" (Luke 21:4). The attending priests, of course, will notice the gifts from those who bring much, but they will not notice hers. Only Jesus does. And He sees much else.

Because Jesus notices, this poor widow becomes an object lesson for ultimate sacrifice, ultimate devotion, ultimate worship, ultimate discipleship. Her gift reaches into the fabric of her livelihood, her spent storage jars, her bare clothes closet, her empty cupboards, her bed made lonely by her husband's death. Her gift strikes at her inability to provide for herself even in the most basic ways: "She of her penury hath cast in all the living that she had" (v. 4).

There are times in our lives where we feel we have nothing more to give, that we have reached the bottom of our empty coffers, whether it is spiritually, physically, mentally, or financially. What we give at this low point is akin to the poor widow in the temple. She essentially has nothing beyond what might sustain her for another day or week. Yet she knows what the Lord requires of her and that she is to give as He has graciously given to her.

The Savior gives us everything, even the most precious of all gifts: His life for our salvation. When we give our very last at our lowest point, despite our "poorness," it is then that the Savior can truly lift us up and call us a true divine worshiper who gives all in His name. [17]

Scriptures referencing the widow: Mark 12:41–44; Luke 21:1–4.

Woman with an Issue of Blood

And, behold, a woman, which was diseased with an issue of blood twelve years, came behind him, and touched the hem of his garment.
(Matthew 9:20)

ON ONE OCCASION, NOT FAR from Capernaum, a number of diseased people reach out to touch Jesus and experience total recovery: "The whole multitude [of the sick] sought to touch him: for there went virtue out of him, and healed them all" (Luke 6:19; see also Matthew 14:35–36). Over time, the woman of our story must hear about this remarkable experience, and rolling it over and over in her mind, she comes to the conclusion that she too must reach out to touch the Savior. At last, opportunity presents itself as He strides through her town, surrounded by others, a circumstance that's not ideal but is enough to embolden her.

Only a woman driven by deep despair and a well of faith would plunge into the midst of a crowd of males and make her way to Jesus, who, jostled on every side, walks in the middle of a tightly packed group through narrow streets in Capernaum. The woman who has suffered from "an issue of blood twelve years" (Matthew 9:20; Mark 5:25) sees no other option. She "had suffered many things of many physicians, and had spent all that she had, and was nothing bettered, but rather grew worse" (Mark 5:26). Now, completely without any other resource, she figuratively throws herself on the mercy of the Savior.

She must know she is unclean and that she could contaminate everyone she brushes against (see Leviticus 15:25–31). But the courage she musters is astounding. Like many of us, she takes a great risk in displaying her faith for all to see. She believes so strongly that the Savior will have an answer to her horrible illness that she presses forward despite the rejection and snubbing she will likely receive from others.

When she finally touches "the border of his garment . . . immediately her issue of blood stanched" (Luke 8:44). In that instant, "she felt in her body that she was healed of that plague" (Mark 5:29). Her desperate act succeeds, bringing sweet relief. She receives healing in its fullness, ending a twelve-year battle. But Jesus does not allow her to retreat. Why? Because everyone in the crowd, both the men who press next to Him and the women who walk on its edge, know the situation with this woman. They know she is unclean and barred from places of worship and, hurtfully, banned from their homes. He wants her healing to be complete and to be known.

So He coaxes her out of the mass of people by asking, "Who touched me?" His question stirs her conscience, as we might expect from her, and "she came trembling, and . . . declared unto him before all the people for what cause she had touched him, and how she was healed immediately" (Luke 8:45–47). Now the secret that she holds is out among her neighbors and acquaintances. They know that she is well. Although she kneels before the Savior, she essentially stands tall among the throng as their equal, no longer marred by ritual uncleanness and physical malady. She is healed not only physically but also socially and spiritually. She is whole, as Jesus affirms: "Thy faith hath made thee whole" (v. 48). Beyond her dreams, as is often the case with us, her faith and prayers are answered.[18]

Notably, some of our challenges may stretch out twelve years or longer, perhaps lasting a lifetime, but the healing will come, either in this life or in the resurrection. And the healing will be complete, just as the woman with the issue of blood.

Scriptures referencing the woman with the issue of blood:
Matthew 9:20–22; Mark 5:25–34; Luke 8:43–48.

Eve, Our First Mother

And Adam called his wife's name Eve; because she was the mother of all living. (Genesis 3:20)

Eve, the "the mother of all living," is the first woman on earth (Moses 4:26). From the beginning of her creation, she lives a life of prayer and worship in the Garden as she and Adam converse with the Lord and receive His instruction. She is the last to be created, after light and darkness, the land and sea, the vegetation and fruit, and all creatures. One of Eve's first worshipful acts is when she is given to Adam as his wife and they are bound by the covenant of celestial marriage: "'Bone of my bones, and flesh of my flesh'" (Genesis 2:23).[19] In this sense, they become the first man and woman "sealed together for eternity."[20]

When we look at eternal marriage as a worshipful act, it brings more reverence to the temple sealing that happens on earth. Through Eve's marriage to Adam, she enters into an important covenant with the Lord, that of being sealed for eternity and making additional promises.

Yet, to satisfy *all* of God's commandments and worship Him as an obedient daughter of God, Eve must take the next step in order to fulfill her divine calling—to bring about the human race. The Lord makes His commandment clear when we read, "And I, God, blessed them, and said unto them: Be fruitful, and multiply, and replenish the earth" (Moses 2:28). Notice how the Lord says He is *blessing* them with this commandment. If Eve will but worship God by following His commandments, then part of the worship includes bearing children, even when it is occasioned by the Fall.

Out of the many notable events in the history of mankind, the Fall single-handedly affects "everyone in the human family."[21] Standing as a buttress to our Savior's Atonement, Eve's divinely led decision becomes the fulfillment of her calling, the ultimate in worship practices, and her "supreme gift to mankind, the opportunity of life on this earth, resulted from her choice to become mortal."[22]

Due to her worshipful and prayerful nature, she has a godlike grasp of her situation, demonstrated in this line: "When [Eve] saw that the tree was good for food" (Moses 4:12). The word *saw* is divinely and grammatically akin to God's "acts of seeing," meaning that when she looks at the tree of good and evil, she sees as God sees and understands her divine duty.[23]

Our perspectives can soften and become more tolerant and loving when we see things as the Lord sees them. Our understanding can also deepen, and our hope can be strengthened. But in order to see as the Lord sees, we need to become more like Him through prayer and worship, just as Eve.

The courage that Eve has didn't come from herself but from the Lord and from her diligence in emulating Him through worship. Every prophet of God recognizes Eve and her divine role as a noble daughter, and she can be held up as an example of faithfulness for men and women everywhere. As a woman who makes a courageous choice in the Garden, Eve continues to call upon the Lord in all things (see Moses 5:4). Obtaining faith and courage through prayer is not a one-time event for her but a lifetime pursuit.

Even with the experiences Eve has in the Garden through conversing with the Lord on a personal basis, she must continue in her diligence.

Once she leaves the Garden, Eve worships the Lord, teaching her children as well: "Adam and Eve blessed the name of God, and they made all things known unto their sons and their daughters" (v. 12). She is already in the good habit of righteous worship and prayer so that even when Satan comes "among them," they "ceased not to call upon God" (v. 13, 16).

Of course, we also understand that exact observance does not guarantee a life free from trials and heartaches. Eve does not enjoy an ideal family life, and more than one of her children prove to be burdensome challenges. Despite her faithful worshiping and her commitment to teach her children in righteousness, she is not exempt from physical or emotional pain. Turning to the Lord in prayer and worship in times of sorrow, as well as rejoicing and gratitude, is what keeps Eve on the path to eternal life and its divine rewards.

Millennia later, her mortal faithfulness is still celebrated in modern scripture. The prophet Joseph F. Smith, who sees Eve in a vision, describes her in honorable tones: "Among the great and mighty ones who were assembled in this vast congregation of the righteous . . . [was] our glorious Mother Eve, with many of her faithful daughters who had lived through the ages and worshiped the true and living God" (D&C 138:39).

Like Eve, from the beginning and continually through all parts of our lives, we must continue in faith. As we worship the Lord, we will take on the mantle of divinity. We can well learn from Eve's steady but unspectacular faithfulness in and her proper worship of the God she knows. Her glorious reward comes to her in heaven, just as it will for each of us.

Scriptures referencing Eve: Genesis 2:21–22; 3; 4:1, 25; 2 Corinthians 11:3; 1 Timothy 2:13; Moses 4:26; 5:11; 1 Nephi 5:11.

Hannah, a Barren Woman

And he had two wives; the name of the one was Hannah, and the name of the other Peninnah: and Peninnah had children, but Hannah had no children. (1 Samuel 1:2)

HANNAH, MEANING "GRACE," IS THE mother of Samuel and a plural wife of Elkanah. His other wife, Peninnah, has children, but Hannah finds herself distressingly barren for many years. It's a challenge that can be heartbreaking and can leave a woman feeling lonely and bereft. In Hannah's case, she doesn't have medical knowledge about why she is barren and may consider it a curse, making the trial devastating in more ways than one.

If a woman is barren during biblical times, she is also subject to divorce. For her, it would be a disgrace to be sent back to her family for any reason, especially barrenness. Fortunately for Hannah, her husband loves her and does not put her away. Still, Hannah desires a child more than anything else, so much so that during a temple visit with her husband, she spends her time weeping and fasting and praying to the Lord (see 1 Samuel 1:7).

When Elkanah discovers her state of grief, he says, "Hannah, why weepest thou? and why eatest thou not? and why is thy heart grieved? am not I better to thee than ten sons?" (v. 8). Elkanah's reasoning convinces Hannah to start eating again, but her heart is still heavy. She continues her prayer and worship by petitioning the Lord at the temple, but she is so despondent that when Eli the priest finds her in a state of "bitterness of soul," he thinks her drunk (vv. 10, 15).

Hannah explains to Eli that she possesses a "sorrowful spirit" (v. 15) and tells him of her supplication to the Lord: "O Lord of hosts, if thou wilt . . . give unto thine handmaid a man child, then I will give him unto the Lord all the days of his life, and there shall be no razor come upon his head" (v. 11).

In this manner, Hannah promises the Lord that she'll offer a great sacrifice as part of her worship of Him if He but grants her the blessing of a child. Like Hannah, many of us may make promises to the Lord, hoping and pleading to receive a specific blessing. It is not unusual or uncommon that when our will is aligned with the Lord's, we are granted our sought-after blessing.

In Hannah's story, it is to her great relief that Eli's responds, "Go in peace: and the God of Israel grant thee thy petition" (v. 17). Hannah knows her prayers have been answered, which is apparent in her recorded actions: she "did eat, and her countenance was no more sad" (v. 18).

True to Eli's prophesy, the Lord answers Hannah's prayers and rewards her diligent worship when she conceives and delivers a son, Samuel. Not forgetting her promise, or bargain, with the Lord, Hannah is faithful in her covenant to give her son back to the Lord. When Samuel is about the age of three and is weaned, Hannah takes him to serve in the temple. Presenting him to Eli, she says, "For this child I have prayed; and the Lord hath given me my petition . . . as long as he liveth he shall be lent to the Lord" (vv. 27–28).

This act is significant to think about. Not only does Hannah deliver her three-year-old child into service at the temple, but she also keeps her covenant to the Lord. Hannah's commitment to her promise doesn't bring the deep sadness we might expect from a mother parting with her young son. Instead, Hannah recognizes the Lord's hand in Samuel's very existence and that his life was granted through her prayers and mighty worship. Although her heart certainly experiences the bittersweet, jangled feelings of separating from Samuel, her joy is evident when she praises the Lord in a song of thanksgiving (see 1 Samuel 2:1–10).[24] Also significant about Hannah's song of thanksgiving is that it includes the first reference in all of scripture to the title Messiah when Hannah calls Christ "his anointed" (v. 10).

With profound gratitude in her heart, Hannah continues in her prayers and worship of the Lord, and each year, she visits Samuel in the temple, bringing "him a little coat" (v. 2:19). She and her husband are dedicated worshipers and "offer the yearly sacrifice" (v. 19). Because of all that Hannah has done, Eli the priest further blesses her husband and her when he says, "The Lord give thee seed of this woman for the loan which is leant to the Lord" (v. 20). This blessing leads to Hannah's conceiving and bearing three more sons and two daughters (see v. 21).

Hannah's story underscores her continuing and unflinching faith in God through prayer and worship. In her situation, her barrenness is lifted during her lifetime, and her grief and despondency are assuaged. Yet we know that many women will not have this wholeness come to them during their earthly life. This does not mean the Lord is any less mindful or full of love for a barren woman or an unmarried woman. We can be assured that "all things must come to pass in their time" (D&C 64:32). Whether a woman is a mother in the physical sense or a mother to those she teaches and serves, she is "laying the foundation of a great work" (v. 33).

We all must remain faithful and continue to worship the Lord. We can be assured that "they who keep their second estate shall have glory added upon their heads for ever and ever" (Abr. 3:26).

Scriptures referencing Hannah: 1 Samuel 1:2–2:21.

Abish, a Lamanite Servant

And it came to pass that they did call on the name of the Lord, in their might, even until they had all fallen to the earth, save it were one of the Lamanitish women, whose name was Abish. (Alma 19:16)

BEHIND CLOSED CURTAINS, IN THE deep of night, when no one can see. These are the only conditions that will allow Abish, a servant to the Lamanite queen, to worship the Lord. For many years, Abish keeps her conversion to the true gospel a secret. First, because it involves the same God the Nephites worship, and she lives among Lamanites. Second, because the people in the land of Ishmael can worship only what the high king allows them to worship. And Abish's own king, Lamoni, is under the jurisdiction of his father.

Some of us may live in situations where we must pray or worship in secret. Perhaps some live in an oppressive country or an oppressive home, and when they want to discuss the things of their hearts, they are restricted. Or perhaps our families don't share our views or love of the gospel, and we need to tread carefully in what we say. Abish knows these dilemmas well, and she lives them for years.

How is it that she possesses a testimony of the Lord in a land of virtually forced religious idol worship?[25] In Alma, we learn the knowledge comes from her father, resulting in Abish having "been converted unto the Lord for many years, on account of a remarkable vision of her father" (Alma 19:16). Assuming this means her earthly father, it seems that he is no longer living, yet Abish still carries the seed of faith in her heart.

When the Nephite missionary Ammon arrives and teaches the plan of salvation to her mistress's husband, King Lamoni, Abish is able to share her beliefs with her people (see Alma 18–19). Surely this is a remarkable moment for her, and perhaps she has been praying for a long time for this day to arrive. Not only do the king and the queen convert to the true gospel, but Abish can now share her testimony with her friends and loved ones too.

When she spends three days hearing speculation about whether or not the king is dead after he falls into an unconscious state while listening to Ammon's message, she's not able to say a word (see Alma 18:41–42). This puts Abish in another tough situation, where she knows the answer but isn't in a position or doesn't have the clearance from the Lord to answer it yet. It's no stretch to imagine Abish's fervent prayers during these three days of uncertainty.

This reminds us of those times when we know the answer or know what's best for a child or family member but must wait before inserting our opinion. We need to rely on the Lord to step in and inspire the person seeking for an answer. Similarly, we can testify of the Church to our children and others around us, yet they still need to discover their own testimony and receive their own confirmation from the Lord.

As a servant to the queen, Abish is in a position to spend time with the queen and be in close confidence. Perhaps Abish uses the opportunity to comfort the queen while at the same time encouraging her to seek out Ammon's help. By this time, Abish has come to know that Ammon is the "prophet of a holy God" (Alma 19:4), as her queen eventually learns as well. This knowledge, acquired because of Abish's refined spiritual sensitivities, allows her to act when the Lord needs her to take action.

When many of the Lamanites in the king's court are incapacitated by the Spirit, Abish recognizes the influence of the Lord: "When she saw that all the servants of Lamoni had fallen to the earth, and also her mistress, the queen, and the king, and Ammon lay prostrate upon the earth, she knew it was the power of God" (v. 17).

We know little of this woman, but her quick actions in a crisis illuminate her inner nature and her preparation through righteous worship and prayer. So it is that, finally, Abish is given the chance to act upon her long-hidden faith: "She ran forth from house to house making it known unto the people" (v. 17). Yet her assignment is not over. When she returns to the palace and sees that fear has descended upon the crowd, she is "exceedingly sorrowful, even unto tears" (v. 28). But instead of cowering, she takes action, hurrying to the unconscious queen's side and taking her hand. At Abish's touch, the queen rises and "clasped her hands, being filled with joy, speaking many words which were not understood" (v. 30).

Abish has prepared herself through prayer and worship to become an instrument in the Lord's hands when her testimony is sorely needed among her queen's people. Her preparation and timely participation in the events that surround the first blossoms of conversion among the Lamanite people is the precursor to a major apex in the Book of Mormon. From this point on, the Lamanites become more spiritual, and the Nephites become less.[26]

As an unforgettable, pivotal witness, Abish demonstrates how a mere servant can exact much influence if she is prepared. And prepared she is, even after a lifetime of secretive worship and prayer. Her faith and fidelity do not need a stage. Today, some of us find ourselves in a similar situation. The Lord is mindful of us, and if we continue in our faithfulness and diligence, we will be prepared when, and if, the time comes to testify of Him. The Savior clarifies, "He that is least among you all, the same shall be great" (Luke 9:48).

Scriptures referencing Abish: Alma 19:16–29.

Section Three
Prophetesses

THE SPIRIT OF PROPHECY IS a gift of the Spirit (see Moroni 10:13). James E. Talmage makes it clear that "no special ordination in the Priesthood is essential to man's receiving the gift of prophecy. . . . The ministrations of Miriam and Deborah show that this gift may be possessed by women also."27 This is reiterated in Articles of Faith 1:7: "We believe in the gift of tongues, prophecy, revelation, visions, healing, interpretation of tongues, and so forth."

Women were allowed to worship publicly in ancient times but only to a certain extent. However, within their realm of worship, throughout scripture, we find examples of women who enjoy the gift of prophecy, whereby they speak for God and their words of prophecy are realized. We refer to these women as prophetesses, and they speak to numbers of people on behalf of the Lord. In this way, women fulfill an additional important role, even though they do not preside at the ancient altars or hold offices of the priesthood.

Other religious activities women participate in during early biblical days include services for the tabernacles (temples) that are performed outside of these structures, such as contributing valuables toward the construction (see Exodus 35:22), spinning colorful yarn and fine linen for sacred fabrics (see v. 25), and assembling the brass from looking glasses for a bronze basin and stand (see Exodus 38:8). The Bible clearly shows that men are in charge of the ritual activities (see Genesis 22, 26, 28), yet women are involved in the essential religious role of prophecy.28

The spirit of prophecy proves to be significant. Many women throughout history have enjoyed this gift, including Miriam, sister of

Moses (see Exodus 15:20); Deborah, a judge in Israel (see Judges 4:4); Huldah, who lives in Jerusalem during Lehi's era (see 2 Chronicles 34:22); Anna, an aged widow at the time of the Savior's birth (see Luke 2:36); Isaiah's wife (see Isaiah 8:3); Noadiah (see Nehemiah 6:14); Elisabeth, mother of John the Baptist (see Luke 1); and Philip's daughters (see Acts 21:9).

Miriam, Prophetess and Sister of Moses

And Miriam the prophetess, the sister of Aaron, took a timbrel in her hand; and all the women went out after her with timbrels and with dances. And Miriam answered them, Sing ye to the Lord, for he hath triumphed gloriously. (Exodus 15:20)

MIRIAM, WHOSE NAME MEANS "EXALTED," is the older sister of Moses. She is witness to miraculous events in her life, which act as precursors to her role as a prophetess. As a young girl, she accompanies her mother, Jochebed, when they send Moses off in a small ark on the Nile River in order to spare his life from the Pharaoh's edict to kill all the sons born to Hebrew women (see Exodus 1:16; 2:4–5). Likely both nervous and excited, Miriam follows the tar-coated ark and keeps an eye on its location as it floats along the river. She hides to watch over her brother until Pharaoh's daughter finds the babe.

This discovery by the Pharaoh's daughter may strike Miriam as divine intervention from the Lord, and in addition, she does everything she can to ensure that her brother will be well taken care of. Miriam secures Jochebed's role of wet nurse for young Moses, keeping child and birth mother together for two or possibly three more years.[29] Miriam must know these events are no coincidence and that the Lord is mindful of her family and her.

At a young age, Miriam already has an instinct for protecting her family and a great love for her brother. Her nurturing personality is plain. Some women seem to be born with a great capacity for compassion, whereas other women find that it takes quite a bit of effort and courage to act accordingly.

It seems that Miriam's innate sensitivity to spiritual matters leads to her being called "a prophetess," although none of her actual prophecies or utterances are preserved in the scriptural text (see Exodus 15:20). Even though she enjoys this type of gift, she must still live righteously and keep herself pure in order to serve as a vessel through which the Lord can speak to His people. Following the children of Israel's deliverance from Egypt, Miriam is a leader among the women and encourages them to celebrate their escape from the Pharaoh and his soldiers. It's evident that the obedience demonstrated in her childhood continues into womanhood.

Miriam takes a timbrel, a musical instrument similar to a small hand drum, and "all the women went out after her with timbrels and with dances" (Exodus 15:20). The women sing and dance together, playing their timbrels in praise of the Lord's deliverance of the children of Israel with Miriam's encouragement: "Sing ye to the Lord, for he hath triumphed gloriously; the horse and his rider hath he thrown into the sea" (v. 21). This form of grateful worship is an important activity for these women to show their gratitude and devotion to the Lord.

As a leader in her community, Miriam also guides her people in prayers and songs of thanksgiving. This concept of gratitude can be repeated in our own families and wards as we recognize the blessings the Lord so generously pours out. In Miriam's life, music is a wonderful and effective way to praise the Lord. Similarly in our own lives, beautiful music can touch our hearts and minds.

In many of the events throughout scripture, gratitude is expressed through songs of praise, or prayer-songs. For example, Hannah praises the Lord when she presents her son, Samuel, for service in the tabernacle. Also, Mary sings a psalm of thanksgiving, known as the "Magnificat," following Elisabeth's blessing (see Luke 1:46–55). It's plain that music often brings the Spirit of the Lord into a group of worshipers (see 2 Kings 3:15; Mark 14:26; D&C 136:28).

Like many of us, Miriam is opinionated and not afraid to speak her mind. She is also not perfect, even though she is well acquainted with the Lord's ways. She and her brother Aaron speak against Moses for marrying an Ethiopian woman (see Numbers 12:1).[30] This raises the Lord's ire, perhaps because He endorses the marriage, and the Lord quickly reprimands Miriam and Aaron. In an extreme move, the Lord afflicts Miriam with leprosy (see v. 10). Aaron appeals to Moses, who in turn appeals to the Lord on behalf of his sister, saying, "Heal her now, O God, I beseech thee" (v. 13). The Lord agrees to withdraw the affliction after seven days. This is a strong lesson for Miriam, and there are no more records of complaints against her sister-in-law.

It seems that even with the status of a prophetess, Miriam is not exempt from censure, as is also the case with many other prophets and prophetesses. Just as a loving parent disciplines their children, the Lord disciplines Miriam for speaking ill of her brother and sister-in-law. In our day, as women serve their own families and those in their communities, there are times when discipline is necessary. There are times when *we* are the ones who need discipline and times when we are the ones to dole it out. But we must keep in mind that "whom the Lord loveth he chasteneth" (Hebrews 12:6). The Lord will not lead us astray, and He will correct us when necessary.

Miriam is certainly a remarkable woman, one who is raised in a slave camp and faces deprivation all her life. Yet the Lord teaches her to be a leader and spokesperson for her people, particularly among other Israelite women. She does not turn her back on the Lord when He censures her but repents and humbles herself, continuing on her divine path.

After a full life of service and leadership and influence, Miriam dies in Kadesh and is buried there (see Numbers 20:1). During this same time, Moses's congregation complains about the lack of water (v. 2–3). Scholars draw a parallel between "Miriam's well"—in which the people are blessed with water while Miriam lives—and the absence of water upon her death, a fitting symbolic honor for this woman's ability to bless her people through her divine lifestyle and willingness to take on the mantle of prophetess.[31]

Like Miriam, even though we need to be chastened and humbled from time to time, the Lord still loves us. Because He is willing to continually teach, uplift, and guide us, it demonstrates our divine value to Him. We need to remember that our successes as well as our stumblings become an example to those around us, and if we continue to rise after we fall, our influence will be that much greater.

Scriptures referencing Miriam: Exodus 2:4–8; 15:20–21; Numbers 12:1–15; 20:1; 26:59; Deuteronomy 24:9; 1 Chronicles 4:17; 6:3; Micah 6:4.

Deborah, Prophetess and Judge in Israel

And Deborah, a prophetess, the wife of Lapidoth, she judged Israel at that time. (Judges 4:4)

THE OLD TESTAMENT DEVOTES NEARLY two chapters to Deborah's prophesies, psalms, and activities. Her position is made clear in the scriptures as she is called a prophetess: "And Deborah, a prophetess, the wife of Lapidoth, she judged Israel at that time" (Judges 4:4). Another declaration of her status is found in the definition of a prophet in Deuteronomy 18:18–21, as Deborah too speaks for God and her words of prophecy are fulfilled.

From these references, Deborah is painted as an extraordinary woman, one who holds the ear of the Lord and is empowered to speak in His behalf to her people. Not only is Deborah a spokeswoman for the Lord, but she also holds an esteemed position in her land. She spends her time between Ramah and Beth-el in Mount Ephraim, where she acts as a judge to the children of Israel (see Judges 4:5). What does this mean exactly? It means that her people look to her to help solve personal and property disputes, to offer guidance in matters of faith, and to lead out in defending her people against their enemies.

This is an interesting occupation in this era for a woman, but apparently, it's not unheard of. It's also an important position, one Deborah takes seriously as she consults with the Lord in making her judgments. In fact, Deborah refers to herself as "a mother in Israel," which can means she's a literal mother with children, but in the broader perspective, it can also mean she is a protector and caretaker of her people during the Canaanite repression (v. 7).

Seeing her role as a judge as akin to being a mother to her people is a fascinating concept. If we view our roles in employment and Church service the same as we do our parenting, perhaps our idea of stewardship would be elevated. We may see the people we work with and serve with as children of our Heavenly Father and as children we can nurture as a mother nurtures.

One of Deborah's prophecies is spelled out when she makes motions to deliver her people from Canaanite control. She summons the Israelite commander Barak and says, "Hath not the Lord God of Israel commanded, saying, Go and draw toward mount Tabor, and take with thee ten thousand men . . . ? And I will draw unto thee . . . the captain of Jabin's army [from Hazor], with his chariots and his multitude; and I will deliver him into thine hand" (vv. 6–7). With the Lord's assurance, Deborah promises Barak that his army will be delivered.

Despite Deborah's reassuring prophesy, Barak tells her, "If thou wilt go with me, then I will go: but if thou wilt not go with me, then I will not go" (v. 8). He refuses to be the leader of the rebellion without Deborah at his side. This signals the influence and comfort she brings to her people, as well as shows her fine reputation. It also attests to the fact that Barak insists on having a spiritual leader with him in a dangerous situation and demonstrates that in this time of political unrest, Israel may lack proper priesthood leadership. It's also clear that Deborah is educated in politics, culture, and the history of her land and people. Deborah, of course, leaves her home to aid Barak in his leadership and makes the journey to bring together the various tribes to fight as one.[32]

In relationship to the battle against the Canaanites, Deborah prophesies that Sisera, the Canaanite chief, will be killed because "the Lord shall sell Sisera into the hand of a woman" (v. 9). Sisera's death will lead to the deliverance of her people from his clutches. Deborah's people are indeed delivered when Jael, the wife of Heber the Kenite, slays Sisera in his sleep (see vv. 17–21) and the Canaanite chariots are swamped in a downpour near Mount Tabor (see Judges 5:21).

Deborah also speaks prophetically about the mother of the executed Sisera, envisioning her as she looks out her window and cries "through the lattice, 'Why is his chariot so long in coming? why tarry the wheels of his chariots?'" (v. 28). We can indeed visualize how the mother of Sisera grieves when she realizes her son is not coming home. This shows Deborah's sympathy as well as her divine connection to the Lord. Even though her people are finally set free, she still has a mother's heart and understands the grief her enemies will face.

In all, this stately woman from the south of her country has an enormous impact on those who live under threat in the north. Through her willingness to extend herself by leaving the comfort and security of her home near Jerusalem and accompanying Barak and his army into Galilee, she helps turn the tide of Canaanite repression and offers her people a brighter future.

Because Deborah devotes herself to serving her people and her country, the Lord blesses her with gifts of prophecy and leadership. Likewise, each of us has specific gifts from the Lord, and we can cultivate and discover through prayer how the Lord would like us to use them. We may not lead a nation into freedom from oppression, but we will have the opportunity to bring many freeing blessings into our lives and the lives of those around us as we live and emulate the gospel.

Scriptures referencing Deborah: Judges 4; Judges 5.

Huldah, Prophetess at the Time of Jerusalem's First Temple

And Hilkiah, and they that the king had appointed, went to Huldah the prophetess. (2 Chronicles 34:22)

HULDAH LIVES IN JERUSALEM DURING a volatile era when the Assyrian Empire is failing and "the Egyptians and the Babylonians are fighting for control."[33] She is a prophetess during the first temple period and, specifically, during King Josiah's reign.[34]

King Josiah has allowed idol worship to infiltrate his kingdom, so Huldah's job as a prophetess of the true Lord proves to be more difficult since the king of the land is not in favor of monotheism. Like other women in the scriptures and many women during our time, Huldah lives in a situation in which those around her are not acting in accordance with the gospel. No doubt her prayers for her land and her people are centered on bringing Jerusalem and her people back to the truth.

The Lord sees fit to provide a way for this to happen, and during the renovation of the temple, scrolls of scripture are found—evidently the book of Deuteronomy, or an early version of it (see 2 Chronicles 34:14–15). This recovered scripture becomes a turning point, and Huldah is a witness to Josiah's future actions of purging idol worship.

When King Josiah reads the newly discovered scriptures that chastise idol worshipers, he becomes worried that his people, who have been heavily embroiled in idol worship, cannot obtain forgiveness and salvation. The king asks his courtiers to find out what is in store for his kingdom—a kingdom that has been neglecting its God. Rightly so, King Josiah is concerned with not only his fate but especially that of his people. He consults the prophetess Huldah, who enjoys a reputation for honesty and trustworthiness.

Huldah's prayers have been answered, and she is given the opportunity to validate the sacred scrolls and their message. Just as Deborah the prophetess, Huldah speaks in the name of God as she begins her prophecy: "Thus saith the Lord God of Israel" (2 Kings. 22:15). This verification means that Huldah's predictions likely influence the eventual inclusion of the text of Deuteronomy in the Bible.[35]

Although under inspiration, Huldah's news is not all happy. She relays the message that the curses recorded in the recovered scroll will indeed happen and the Lord "will bring evil upon this place, and upon the inhabitants thereof . . . therefore [the Lord's] wrath shall be poured out upon this place, and shall not be quenched" (2 Chronicles 34:24–25).

As terrible as this pronouncement is, the Lord extends some mercy to King Josiah based on the efforts he has already begun to make. Huldah prophetically clarifies, "Because thine heart was tender, and thou didst humble thyself before God . . . and didst rend thy clothes, and weep before me . . . thou shalt be gathered to thy grave in peace" (vv. 27–28). This is a great example of the Lord's mercy and justice. Even when we repent of our sins, there are still consequences to pay that follow the Lord's execution of justice. Huldah well knows this, and part of her prophetess role is to pass on the information to Josiah.

Trusting in Huldah's prophecy, King Josiah takes it upon himself to go to the temple to read the words from the scroll. In front of the gathered "men of Judah, and the inhabitants of Jerusalem, and the priests, and the Levites, and all the people, great and small" (v. 30), Josiah makes a covenant before the Lord to walk after Him and to keep His commandments "with all his heart, and with all his soul" (v. 31). He is so passionate about his covenant that he persuades all those in Jerusalem and Benjamin to make the same promises.

Through hearkening to Huldah's counsel and undergoing a change of heart, Josiah turns his life around. There have most likely been times in our lives when the prophet's words have pierced our souls and effected a change in our hearts. Following the counsel of our Church leaders can bring us closer to the Lord and give us peace in our challenges, as demonstrated by King Josiah.

Huldah's prophecy is further fulfilled when "all [Josiah's] days they departed not from following the Lord" (v. 33). King Josiah remains faithful, illustrating that he's had a true change of heart. When he suffers from mortal wounds sustained in a battle against Pharaoh Neco at Megiddo, he dies with peace in his soul, knowing he did all he could to save his people.[36]

This is really all we can ask of the Lord as we live our lives in righteousness. The storms of tribulation will surely rage around us, we will pay consequences for sin, and we'll endure some regrets, but if we turn our hearts to the Lord, we will have peace.

At the time of her prophecy, Huldah may not have realized the long-term effect it would have. But her faithfulness as a daughter of God becomes a key in His hands as she helps both to rid her people of idol worship and to shape the text of future recorded scripture. Because Huldah prays for her people and serves the true Lord, she becomes a divine instrument in His hands.

We may wonder what fruits *our* faithfulness might bring. How will our Sabbath day observance, tithe paying, scripture study, and observance of temple covenants culminate in something as grand as saving a generation from idol worship? Today, there are many forms of idol worship that draw us and our families away from things of the Spirit. Putting the Lord before all idols establishes a house of God. As we remember that the small, simple things do matter, we can find comfort in the Lord's promise: "By small and simple things are great things brought to pass" (Alma 37:6).

Scriptures referencing Huldah:
2 Chronicles 34:22–28; 2 Kings 22:14–20.

Anna, Prophetess in Jerusalem

And there was one Anna, a prophetess, the daughter of Phanuel, of the tribe of Aser: she was of a great age, and had lived with an husband seven years from her virginity. (Luke 2:36)

THE PROPHETESS ANNA LIVES DURING the time of Christ. Her name is the New Testament form of Hannah, and she is the only woman called a prophetess in the Gospels. What a remarkable era to live in, and Anna is there front and center. Her family history descends from the tribe of Asher, in which she is the daughter of Phanuel.

Unfortunately, Anna becomes a widow after a seven-year marriage, and there is no mention of whether or not she has children. She is, therefore, a woman whose life takes an unexpected turn. But as we will learn, Anna continues in her devotion to the Lord and determines to serve Him all the remainder of her days.

In our time, we find women like Anna, women who have gone through difficult challenges yet continue in their pure devotion. Anna is a testament to modern women that it's possible to live a life of joy even when struck with a severe trial. Anna carries an eternal perspective in her heart, and it's no small matter that she is heralded as a prophetess—one who draws close to the Lord and gains His utmost trust.

Interestingly enough, she never remarries but instead spends her remaining widowhood serving in the temple—service estimated at over sixty years. It's an impressive record of service in the public eye. Not all women are able to perform such a service away from home and for the public. Yet, chances are, they are in service the majority of the time, whether it be at home, in the workplace outside the home, or in a Church calling. Notably, Anna's devotion in her calling spans a lifetime. Clearly, she has the desire and ability to serve in the temple, and like many other women, she prioritizes her time so she can be there, likely maintaining a residence near the holy place.

We meet Anna as a woman "of a great age," of fourscore and four years (age 84; Luke 2:37) at the temple on Jesus's presentation day. With the forty days of Mary's required purification after giving birth at an end,[37] she and Joseph bring Jesus into Jerusalem. They are to present their newborn son to the Lord God at the temple, according to the law of Moses. Part of the presentation at the temple is offering a sacrifice of two turtledoves or two young pigeons in order to complete Mary's purification (see Luke 2:24). Simeon first meets Mary and Joseph; he is a man who has been promised that he will not die before seeing the Christ. He greets the parents and takes Jesus into his arms and prophesies about the salvation that has come to earth.

While Mary and Joseph "[marvel] at those things which were spoken" by Simeon (Luke v. 33), Anna enters the scene. Like Simeon, the Spirit leads her to the Christ child and unmistakably informs her that this Infant is the Redeemer.

Upon meeting the Christ child, Anna not only becomes a witness of the Savior, but she also gives "thanks likewise unto the Lord, and [speaks] of him to all them that [look] for redemption in Jerusalem" (v. 38). This notation leads us to believe that after Jesus and His parents flee to Egypt, Anna speaks reverentially about His birth and His presence on earth for as long as she lives. Her testimony may have been great before, as evidenced in her role as prophetess, but now it's magnified as she can serve as a sure witness to the Savior's existence.

In this way, Anna's lifelong devotion to the Lord is no longer based on faith, but like the brother of Jared, she "had faith no longer, for [she] *knew*, nothing doubting" (Ether 3:19, emphasis added). What a wonderful gift and one each of us will gain, either in this life or in the eternities. For now, it is important for us to remember what precedes Anna's sure knowledge and what she embraced for at least sixty years of her life—it is something we cannot see or hear but only feel: faith.

Anna's divinity and role as a prophetess is further secured when we learn that she is the second woman in the Bible noted as fasting other than on the Day of Atonement (Esther is the first; see Esther 4:16). Fasting isn't normally encouraged for women during ancient times, yet it seems that for Anna it was part of her spiritual regimen wherein she "served God with fastings and prayers night and day" (Luke 2:37). It is part of her devotion toward becoming like her divine Father in Heaven, and it is this sort of devotion that leads to the opportunity of meeting the infant Jesus Christ and becoming a physical and spiritual witness to His mission on earth.

Fasting can be difficult for many men and women. For women, pregnancy, breast-feeding, or health issues might prevent a woman from fasting, and there are times when fasting is not possible. This is why there are instances in our lives when we must rely on others who are prayerfully fasting. Anna's fasting is likely no easy task either, but she recognizes the importance of it in bringing her close to the Spirit, and as she continues to fast, her faith is strengthened.

At the age of eighty-four, Anna may not have many more years on earth to testify of Jesus's birth, but she becomes a true witness, and certainly, her unquestionable testimony blesses many lives. Her devotion to the Lord and her people, as well as the spirit of inspiration she cultivates in order to become one of the Lord's spokeswomen, marks her long life as a touching example of a divine woman. Like some of us, her life doesn't turn out how she planned. In Anna's case, her marriage is short and she evidently does not have children, yet she finds ways to reprioritize her life and devote it to the Lord. Instead of feeling sorry for herself, she clearly moves forward with purpose and creates a fulfilling life, giving us a wonderful example.

Scriptures referencing Anna: Luke 2:36–38.

Isaiah's Wife, "the Prophetess"

And I went unto the prophetess; and she conceived, and bare a son.
(Isaiah 8:3)

GIVEN THE HONORIFIC TITLE "THE prophetess" (Isaiah 8:3), this remarkable woman remains unnamed. Whether she raises her voice to prophesy, as her husband Isaiah does, we do not know. But her two sons receive divinely appointed names, a clear signal that the Lord knows who she is and that through her He accomplishes His celestial purposes. As a further marker, the weaning of her second child becomes a sign to the whole country that the Lord will deliver them from their enemies.

Her first son bears the name Shear-jashub, meaning "a remnant shall return." On a fateful morning in 734 BC, hand in hand with his father, this child is led to meet the young King Ahaz and his bodyguards, who, staying just out of bow shot of a pair of invading armies, are inspecting "the conduit of the upper pool" (Isaiah 7:3), an important water source for Jerusalem. This specific appearance of the prophet before the king, with this child in tow, is to assure the monarch and his staff that the Lord will see that only a remnant of the two armies returns home and that He will deliver the people of their city. This experience illustrates that Isaiah and his wife's son and his name serve as signs of the Lord's unending concern for His people.

On this very occasion, while Isaiah and his son stand next to the king, the Lord's Spirit descends on Isaiah, and he utters the prophetic words, "Behold, a virgin shall conceive, and bear a son, and shall call his name Immanuel" (v. 14).

Such unlooked for spiritual moments come to all of us if we are prepared and seek knowledge. Perhaps it will not happen on such a large scale as with this one to Isaiah, his son, and his special wife, though, for this prophecy points in two directions: one, toward the birth of the Son of God in mortality (see Matthew 1:23) and the other toward the birth of the prophetess's second son. We notice that the word translated *virgin* (Hebrew *'almah*) can point to a young woman without specifying her marital status. In its sense as a prophecy about the coming Messiah, Isaiah's utterance reaches across the centuries with the resonating reassurance that God is always with His people (see Alma 19:13), emphasizing the meaning of the name Immanuel. In its other contemporary sense, before the prophetess's expected child is able to eat "butter and honey" and before he knows "to refuse the evil, and choose the good," both of the kings who make war on Judah at this moment will be gone (Isaiah 7:14–16; 8:4).

Not long afterward, the prophetess "conceived, and bare a son" whom she and her husband, under inspiration, call Maher-shalal-hash-baz (Isaiah 8:1–4), a symbolic name that means "swift is the booty, speedy is the prey" (Isaiah 8:1–4). This name too has to do with the Lord's power to deliver, as illustrated in the eventual deliverance of Jerusalem from the grasp of the two invading armies. Thus, in Isaiah's wife's life, whether supporting her husband or bearing and rearing children, heavenly inspiration is everywhere abundant.[38]

Not only is she a witness to one of the greatest prophecies in history, but she is also an example among women of any age as she develops her own spiritual strength, separate from that of her prophet-husband. This is a woman who does not live on borrowed light but finds the sweet, tender mercies of the Lord through her own supplication and devotion and through her concern for her unusual children—a task that is never easy, even if one's husband is a prophet, but a task Isaiah's wife undertakes as she spends a lifetime cultivating her own spiritual aptitude.

Scriptures referencing Isaiah's wife: Isaiah 7–8.

Noadiah, A Prophetess

My God, think thou upon Tobiah and Sanballat according to these their works, and on the prophetess Noadiah, and the rest of the prophets, that would have put me in fear. (Nehemiah 6:14)

THE PROPHETESS NOADIAH MAKES HER appearance in one verse, Nehemiah 6:14. But she is grouped together with a series of other prophets, leading us to believe she is equal in consideration and respect to these men. The tradition of prophets and prophetesses during political upheavals has long been established. Similarly, Noadiah lives during a critical period in Jerusalem, after many Jews have been released from bondage in Babylon. Noadiah will soon cross paths with one of these Jewish exiles, the nobleman Nehemiah.

Like so many prophetesses who have gone before her, Noadiah lives a life of devotion to the Lord. She continually strives for divinity in order to serve as a mouthpiece of the Lord, although it's interesting to note that her role is not one of heralding promised blessings but one of warning.

Having gained the blessing of the Persian king Artaxerxes, the nobleman Nehemiah returns to Jerusalem with the intent of restoring the city fully and securely to the Jews. He is so determined in his goals that he fails to maintain the larger perspective—and this is where we meet the prophetess. Noadiah will become a vehicle of warning to the nobleman. While Nehemiah sets his sights on reconstruction projects, such as rebuilding the walls and gates around the city, trouble starts to develop throughout the land.

When Nehemiah focuses on the reconstruction of Jerusalem's walls, other tribes see it as a warlike maneuver. As a result, he is forced to arm the workers who are rebuilding the wall against nomads and against the Samaritans.[39] The prophetess Noadiah feels compelled to caution Nehemiah about his actions. She understands he's sending a message to Jerusalem's political opponents, which has the potential to stir up old contentions. And with her heart singular to the Lord, she can view the situation with a greater perspective than the nobleman, who is too close to his frantic project.

Noadiah warns Nehemiah about the consequences "that would have put me in fear" as she worries that war will follow (Nehemiah 6:14). Heedless of the prophetess's warning, Nehemiah perseveres in his plans and continues constructing the walls and gates. So where does this leave Noadiah? Ignored by the nobility, yet that does not stop her from prophesying.

This event can easily be compared to parenting and the warnings we give our children—some of them unheeded. If we tell our children to watch out for cars in the street, they can see the wisdom of it immediately as they observe cars speeding past. If we tell our children to choose their friends wisely, it becomes an abstract warning to them, one in which they may not share the same perspective as us.

Noadiah's story also illustrates that it's equally as important to obey the good promptings of the Spirit as it is to listen to the warnings. We may not always know the whys or whats of the warnings we are given. And we may question the validity or motivation of the warning, just as our children may question our warnings to them. But if we do trust in the Lord, just as our children might listen to our warnings, we will be blessed.

In Nehemiah's case, he chooses to see Noadiah's words as politically motivated, and though he ignores her warnings, the prophesies' fulfillments come to pass. In the end, as foreseen by Noadiah, the people of the city soon depart from their covenants.

As the prophetess discovers, sometimes warning people is all we can verbally do. Agency dictates that their choices are their own, and although it may be painful to watch a loved one make a wrong choice, we need to continue along our own faithful paths and not turn away from the Lord in disappointment.

Noadiah accomplishes the tasks the Lord has given her. She doesn't stop her prayers for her people, nor does she falter in her faith. Is she one to question the Lord as to why she's not able to affect the salvation of her own people? Part of the Lord's promise to His people is that He will give us warnings. In this way, Noadiah is fulfilling her divine calling from the Lord. She is teaching her people that the Lord gives His word and keeps it.

In Noadiah's time, she functions as the warning mouthpiece of the Lord. Who holds that position in our lives? How many times have our parents, leaders, or prophets warned us? Have we heeded those warnings? We don't always take warnings seriously, and when we do not, the Lord continues to be merciful. He has provided a way to for us to repent and return to Him through the Atonement. But it does us well to remember that He does not stray from His instruction just because we stray from His path.

Scripture referencing Noadiah: Nehemiah 6:14.

Elisabeth, Mother of John the Baptist

But the angel said unto him, Fear not, Zacharias: for thy prayer is
heard; and thy wife Elisabeth shall bear thee a son, and thou
shalt call his name John. (Luke 1:13)

THE EYE OF GOD ALREADY rests on Elisabeth. In the Jerusalem temple during his once-in-a-lifetime ministration at the incense altar, Elisabeth's husband, Zacharias, sees and hears an angel promising the impossible: that his barren wife, Elisabeth, well past childbearing years, will give birth to a son whom God will send to her.

When Elisabeth is almost six months pregnant, a knock on her door arouses her from her household tasks. Two unexpected experiences clap together, one after the other. First, she is surprised to find her young cousin Mary standing at her door. Second, because Mary brings the Spirit of God and because Elisabeth is preparing spiritually for the birth of her divinely promised child, having "hid herself five months" (Luke 1:24), the Spirit comes upon Elisabeth in a rush. The trigger for this sudden spiritual moment is her unborn son suddenly moving in her womb, and instantly, "Elisabeth was filled with the Holy Ghost" (vv. 41, 44).

Through her past experiences, Elisabeth has learned to put her trust completely in the Lord. She prepares herself, just as we need to continually be prepared, in order to receive the Lord's guidance. When Elisabeth is presented with yet another miracle, she is more than ready to embrace without question the divine event of Mary's miraculous conception.

The divine Spirit gives Elisabeth prophetic utterance, and with divine sight, she calls "with a loud voice," almost singing, "Blessed art thou [Mary] among women, and blessed is the fruit of thy womb." In dramatic fashion, she now knows the secret that Mary alone carries: who the mother of the Son of God is. Elisabeth continues in words that brim with prophetic insight: "Whence is this to me, that the mother of my Lord should come to me?" (vv. 42–43). In a few spoken sentences, Elisabeth becomes what her son will become—the prophetic herald for the Son of God.

In her typically generous way, she turns all attention to her young guest. Under divine influence, Elisabeth prophesies, "Blessed is she [Mary] that believed: for there shall be a performance of those things which were told her from the Lord" (v. 45). And what are "those things which were told her from the Lord"? They are that Mary will "conceive in [her] womb, and bring forth a son" who will "be called the Son of the Highest" (vv. 31–32). What is more, "those things" include the angel's revelation that "the power of the Highest shall overshadow [Mary]: therefore also that holy thing which shall be born of [her] shall be called the Son of God" (v. 35).

Elisabeth's spiritual preparation and nurturing ability allow her to greet her young, unmarried, pregnant cousin and take her into her home with open arms. No judgment passes from Elisabeth's lips; her reaction is simply the spiritual manifestation that can only come from a woman who views her cousin through spiritual eyes. This is a fine example of a woman whose heart is full of charity. Elisabeth does not judge her cousin's condition and views Mary as the Lord views her.

When we take it upon ourselves to see others in the Lord's loving way, our compassion and desire to serve each other increases. For Elisabeth, it results in her own well becoming spiritually and richly filled as she is now the first witness of the virgin conception and therefore understands that Mary's pregnancy is miraculous—as miraculous as her own.[40]

As modern-day miracles occur in our lives, we might at first carry a doubt or question if it comes from the Lord. But as we allow ourselves to receive the Spirit's gentle confirmation, we come to realize that with God, all things are possible in His time and according to His divine plan (see v. 37).

Scriptures referencing Elisabeth: Luke 1:5–25, 39–45, 56–66.

Daughters of Philip

And the next day we that were of Paul's company departed, and came unto Cæsarea: and we entered into the house of Philip the evangelist, which was one of the seven; and abode with him. And the same man had four daughters, virgins, which did prophesy. (Acts 21:8–9)

THE FOUR DAUGHTERS OF PHILIP, who all possess the gift of prophecy (see Acts 21:9), do not figure in the ongoing narrative of scripture. But because of their righteous lives and because of their remarkable gift, they draw Luke's notice when they are residing in Caesarea on the Mediterranean coast, where he meets them and seems impressed: "*We* entered into the house of Philip . . . and abode with him" (v. 8; emphasis added). The daughters' gift fulfills a scriptural promise through the prophet Joel that the Apostle Peter quotes and Luke records: "Your sons and your daughters shall prophesy, and . . . on my servants and on my handmaidens I will pour out in those days of my Spirit: and they shall prophesy" (Acts 2:17–18; Joel 2:28–29).

These young women grow up in Jerusalem, and it's in that city that we first hear of their father as a priesthood leader who serves among the Greek-speaking members of the Church (see Acts 6:5). Hence, they are witnesses not only to the charitable work of their father and his Greek-speaking associates but also to the early ministrations of the Twelve after the Savior's ascension. The older daughters may have met Jesus and then seen Him after His Resurrection, although we cannot be certain. They do meet prominent Church members in Jerusalem during their youth, including Jesus's mother and brothers who remain in the city (see Acts 1:14).

In this manner, the daughters have grown up in a spiritually rich environment, with supreme examples of righteousness surrounding them, but they still have a choice, just as each of us has today, of whether or not to embrace the teachings of Christ for themselves.

Will our choice be similar to the daughters of Philip? Are we willing to put in the time and preparation it takes to reach our divine potential and become as the Lord sees us and serve as He would have us serve? These are decisions each person is faced with as she or he makes the daily choice to take one step closer or one step farther from the light.

In this small example, these daughters become an important, credible source for Luke as he gathers information for his Gospel and book of Acts, not only during the "many days" he stays in their home (Acts 21:10), but also during the two years he resides in Caesarea while the Apostle Paul is under house arrest (see Acts 24:27). The daughters become important witnesses whom Luke interviews, making their stories a fundamental part of his written reports.[41] It's remarkable to consider that their story demonstrates the fulfillment of prophecy as they prophesy themselves, and Luke finds the girls' gifts notable enough to include in his records.

Although our personal stories may not be published in written form by a prominent author, they will be recorded in the annals of heaven. It's also important to record our personal histories because, like the daughters of Philip, our stories of faith may influence generations to come. We may not have an incredible conversion story to share or some publicly witnessed challenge to overcome, but the daughters of Philip are a testament that quietly living the gospel and staying true to our faith is worthy of note in the Lord's eyes.

Scriptures referencing Philip's daughters: Acts 21:8–9.

Section Four
Crossing the Line

SCRIPTURE DRAWS OUR GAZE TO several examples of women who utter wonderful prophecies and who deliver spirituality and knowledge to their people. But with all things, there is an opposite, and it is important for us to understand when the line has been crossed so we can be watchful and wary. Not all women who claim to be prophetesses are preaching the Lord's word. Ezekiel gives us this warning against worldly prophetesses: "Set thy face against the daughters of thy people, which prophesy out of their own heart" (Ezekiel 13:17). In other words, there are those who prophesy not by the Spirit of the Lord but from their *own* hearts and minds, using supposed divine contacts to manipulate people or circumstances.

As witnessed in our modern world, we know that spirituality and prophecy can be manipulated through mediums such as witchcraft, sorceries, and other divinations. All of these mediums have historical examples in both the Bible and the Book of Mormon. Some leaders reign in wickedness, such as King Manasseh, who "caused his children to pass through the fire . . . also he observed times, and used enchantments, and used witchcraft, and dealt with a familiar spirit" (2 Chronicles 33:6). The prophet Mormon points out that the appearance of the evil powers in his day, including "sorceries, and witchcrafts, and magics," are direct fulfillment of Abinadi's and Samuel the Lamanite's well-known prophecies (Mormon 1:19).[42]

Thousands of years later, Joseph F. Smith clarifies that "the gifts of the Spirit and the powers of the holy Priesthood are of God, they are given for the blessing of the people, for their encouragement, and for the strengthening of their faith. This Satan knows full well, therefore he seeks by imitation-miracles to blind and deceive the children of God."[43]

If we can understand when spirituality is being used for ill purposes, we can follow the promptings of the Holy Ghost and steer clear of such manipulations. By reading about women such as Queen Jezebel, who brings idols into Israel (see 1 Kings 18); Rahab, a harlot in Jericho (see Joshua 2); the harlot Isabel, who leads more than just Corianton astray (see Alma 39); and the daughter of King Jared II, who starts a secret combination to assassinate her grandfather Omer (see Ether 8), we discover women who use wickedness to obtain unrighteous powers and dominion, and we come to recognize the evidences of such unholiness around us. We can be assured that the Spirit will warn us, and we will be able to warn others as well.

Spiritual imitation leads nowhere. It is heartbreaking to think that something beautiful and divine can be twisted and made ugly. But this is exactly Lucifer's intention. In fact, the Savior warns us against using power based in evil sources: "Many will say to me in that day, Lord, Lord, have we not prophesied in thy name? and in thy name have cast out devils? and in thy name done many wonderful works? And then will I profess unto them, I never knew you: depart from me, ye that work iniquity" (Matthew 7:22–23).

In addition, Joseph F. Smith says, "There is no power in witchcraft itself, only as it is believed in and accepted."[44] Similarly, the Apostle Paul says that witchcraft is a work of the flesh, not of God (see Galatians 5:19–20). Paul also warns us that "they which do such things shall not inherit the kingdom of God" (v. 21).

Desperation leads to some women consorting with alternate mediums in order to find answers to spiritual questions, but the Savior provides a better way. He is there to guide us, to lead us, to give us peace, and to carry us. He says, "Come unto me, all ye that labour and are heavy laden, and I will give you rest. Take my yoke upon you, and learn of me; for I am meek and lowly in heart: and ye shall find rest unto your souls. For my yoke is easy, and my burden is light" (Matthew 11:28–30).

Jezebel, A Wicked Queen

And Jezebel his wife said unto him, Dost thou now govern the kingdom of Israel? arise, and eat bread, and let thine heart be merry: I will give thee the vineyard of Naboth the Jezreelite. (1 Kings 21:7)

To label Jezebel as a destroying queen and a false prophetess fits the evidence found in scripture. Leading her army into a hopeless battle would have done less damage than introducing false idols into Israel, a practice many foreign biblical queens undertake when they are first introduced into their new kingdoms.

Jezebel's idol worshiping is amassed in the form of 450 prophets of Baal and 400 prophets of "a [sacred] grove" for worship (1 Kings 16:33)—in honor of the goddess Asherah, otherwise known as the queen of heaven.

When King Ahab marries the Phoenician princess Jezebel, daughter of King Ethbaal, Ahab is already in a downward spiral. To change the climate of religious worship in a country whose identity is scarred, at best, in its worship of Jehovah stands as a direct affront to the God who is preserving Israel in the first place.

In 1 Kings 16:31, we learn that Ahab does not waste a moment between marrying Jezebel and worshiping false idols: "He took to wife Jezebel . . . and went and served Baal, and worshipped him." In fact, Jezebel takes it one step further and "cut[s] off the prophets of the Lord" (1 Kings 18:4). In other words, she disenfranchises and then executes them, all save one hundred who the faithful Obadiah is able to hide away (v. 13).

This idol worship introduces a religious plague in King Ahab's country. And in a ghastly turnabout, the new queen hunts down Ahab's own people and executes them for their belief in Jehovah.

Our choices in a spouse may not have consequences of death or the downfall of the religious climate of a country, but choosing someone who does not believe what we do may create marital challenges that can cripple our growth. We know that every marriage encounters trials, but having the Lord's approbation in making such a monumental decision can keep unnecessary grief at bay.

Jezebel is not the only woman to worship the queen of heaven (see Jeremiah 7:18) but is counted among twenty-five others.[45] Undoubtedly, idol worship goes hand in hand with divination and enchantments, in other words, false religious devotion and spirituality. Unfortunately, as idol worship becomes prevalent in a society, the people leave "all the commandments of the Lord their God" (2 Kings 17:16), and in Jezebel's kingdom, they "caused their sons and their daughters to pass through the fire, and used divination and enchantments, and sold themselves to do evil in the sight of the Lord, to provoke him to anger" (v. 17). Jezebel is specifically accused of witchcraft when Jehu answers Joram's inquiry of whether Jehu comes in peace: "What peace, so long as the whoredoms of thy mother Jezebel and her witchcrafts are so many?" (2 Kings 9:22).

Not only does false religious devotion include the worshiper, it also involves the entire family, and the consequences are for ill. Although women are the ones noted for worshiping the queen of heaven in all of her forms and names, goddess worship involves the whole community: "Neither have our kings, our princes, our priests, nor our fathers, kept thy law" (Nehemiah 9:34; see also Jeremiah 44:15–17).

As we see time and time again, the Lord doesn't take kindly to those who cross the lines of false prophecy and divination: "Therefore the Lord was very angry with Israel, and removed them out of his sight" (2 Kings 17:18).[46]

Activities supporting goddess worship include burning incense and pouring drink offerings (see Jeremiah 44:17), weaving rugs and hangings for the worship groves (see 2 Kings 23:7), children gathering wood, fathers kindling the fires, and women kneading dough for their supposed sacred meals (see Jeremiah 7:18), and false prophesying or speaking a "lying divination" (Ezekiel 13:7).

For all of her spiritual debauchery, it's no surprise that Jezebel meets a horrific end. The Lord foretells her death when He speaks to Elijah: "The dogs shall eat Jezebel by the wall of Jezreel" (1 Kings 21:23). This dreadful event comes to pass in this way: "And they went to bury her: but they found no more of her than the skull, and the feet, and the palms of her hands" (2 Kings 9:35).

The insult and affront that Queen Jezebel brings to the land of Israel is such a deep wound in true believers' hearts that Jezebel later becomes a figurative name for a woman who causes "great harm to the Church in Thyatira."[47] In Revelation, we read that the figurative Jezebel, "which calleth herself a prophetess, to teach and to seduce my servants to commit fornication, and to eat things sacrificed unto idols" (2:20) is a person or sect whom the Lord warns us about. Thus, Jezebel remains a symbol of all that false religion can create.

The story of Jezebel becomes a dire warning to us all. Our lives may not end in horrific and violent deaths, but the fate of those who preach against the Lord is serious indeed. Jezebel may have enjoyed a few years of power and reverence from her people, but her lot for eternity is grim. Here, the actions of a single woman given the right amount of power changes a nation and changes lives for the worse.

Scriptures referencing Jezebel: 1 Kings 16:31; 18:4, 13, 19; 19:1–2; 21:5–25; 2 Kings 9; Revelation 2:20.

Rahab, a Harlot

By faith the harlot Rahab perished not with them that believed not, when she had received the spies with peace. (Hebrews 11:31)

RAHAB, HER NAME MEANING "BROAD," plays an integral role in protecting two men who act as spies for Joshua in Jericho. She gains notoriety because her family becomes the only one saved when Joshua and his army burn Jericho to the ground and slay all the people and animals.

We know exactly why the two spies went to Rahab's home in the first place—because strange men going to a harlot's place are not readily noticed. And the two men know a harlot won't turn them away, and the same desperation that drives her to endure a profession such as harlotry leads these men to assume she can be bribed in other ways.

Regardless, she wisely provides a hiding place for them and takes them "up to the roof of the house, and [hides] them with stalks of flax" (Joshua 2:6). After the king's men complete a fruitless search of her home, she tells the spies that she knows "the Lord hath given you the land" (v. 9) because of the stories she's heard about the parting of the Red Sea and the destruction of "the two kings of the Amorites" (v. 10).

Cleverly, she asks the spies she's just protected to return her kindness with a token of their own. She pleads for them to "save alive my father, and my mother, and my brethren, and my sisters, and all that they have, and deliver our lives from death" (v. 13). The spies agree to her demands: "Our life for yours, if ye utter not this our business" (v. 14).

Rahab helps them escape through her window; they climb down a scarlet cord, and Rahab advises them to flee to the mountains, saying, "Hide yourselves there three days" (v. 16). The spies tell her to tie the scarlet thread in her window so when the army returns to destroy the city, they will know to spare the people in her house (see v. 18–19).

Despite Rahab's unsavory occupation, she recognizes what is about to happen to her city and that Joshua comes with the power of the Lord. She is willing to help the Israelite spies, even at danger to herself, because she can see the value in being their ally and realizes that all things can be done with the Lord's help. This demonstration of faith and conversion is reason enough for her to be included in Paul's and James's narratives when they later write that "by faith the harlot Rahab perished not" (Hebrews 11:31; see also James 2:25). Their admiration rests on a woman who, though she follows an odious path, knows when she should respect the servants of the Lord.

Rahab's story is also a testament to the strength of the Lord. The surprising conversion and testimony of Rahab is a momentous event in and of itself when we consider what her lifestyle must be. Her willingness to open her heart and home to the Lord's servants leads to the sparing of her family's lives, a remarkable and merciful blessing. In this vein, we realize that we too are privy to the power and indelible mercy of the Lord. His purpose will go forward. Even a woman in a lowly occupation, usually considered beneath notice, can become an instrument in His hands if she will but open her heart, change her ways, and embrace His goodness.

Scriptures referencing Rahab: Joshua 2:1–21; 6:17, 23, 25; Hebrews 11:31; James 2:25.

Isabel, a Harlot

And this is not all, my son. Thou didst do that which was grievous unto me; for thou didst forsake the ministry, and did go over into the land of Siron among the borders of the Lamanites, after the harlot Isabel.
(Alma 39:3)

THE HARLOT ISABEL APPEARS BY name only once in the Book of Mormon (see Alma 39:3), adding her to the short list of women whose names are cited within the scriptural text. But her influence is enough that Alma the Younger spends several verses warning his son Corianton about her. This leads us to deduce that Isabel is no common harlot. At the very least, she seems to be an influential woman in her city, if not someone with immense power.

The fact that Corianton has to leave his residence and go to the Lamanite town of Siron in order to follow after a harlot alludes to the possibility of Isabel's being a cult leader.[48] This sets Isabel above the ranks of a simple harlot, accelerating her to the position of an idol or goddess whom her devotees worship. Because Corianton "didst forsake the ministry" to follow "after the harlot Isabel" (Alma 39:3), we may believe that whatever desperation led Isabel to harlotry in the first place has now become a viable industry, complete with influential worshipers.

The profession of harlotry is not new to Isabel's day; its appearance is recorded all the way back to Tamar (see Genesis 38:24). But it seems Isabel's brand of harlotry is much more involved and includes idolatry and profane prostitution similar to that described in Jeremiah's narrative,[49] and continues to be mentioned by prophets such as

Abinadi, who preach repentance in King Noah's court: "If ye teach the law of Moses why do ye not keep it? Why do ye set your hearts upon riches? Why do ye commit whoredoms and spend your strength with harlots?" (Mosiah 12:29).

Isabel's ability to draw an influential figure such as Corianton into her lair probably means she has the capability to influence many others—a fact Alma well knows. He strikes at the heart of the matter when he tells Corianton that his actions are "most abominable above all sins save it be the shedding of innocent blood or denying the Holy Ghost" (Alma 39:5). Isabel is no one-time harlot like Tamar but uses her power of influence and temptation to further cripple a civilization that is already well on its way to an awful demise.

In this light, we might consider the following questions: Do we spend hours seeking esteem from others instead of discovering what the Lord wants us to do? Have some of our actions or words or attitudes led others astray? Isabel's actions demonstrate the enormous influence one woman can exercise for good or for ill within a society. With a different choice, she has the potential to follow in Alma the Younger's footsteps, who repents and uses his considerable abilities in a positive way. Although the scriptural account does not mention her journey toward redemption, we can be assured that if she chooses to repent, the Savior will extend His redemption to her just as He does to each of us. Isabel's choices and alluring influence thwart many from the path that leads to celestial spheres, making their choices a matter of grave personal consequence. With this in mind, we must proceed with care in our individual choices.

Scriptures referencing Isabel: Alma 39:3–4, 11.

Daughter of King Jared II

Now the daughter of Jared being exceedingly expert, and seeing the sorrows of her father, thought to devise a plan whereby she could redeem the kingdom unto her father. (Ether 8:8)

IT MAY COME AS NO surprise that women in the book of Ether become involved in the many secret combinations designed to overthrow kings and rearrange kingdoms. The daughter of Jared II [50] becomes the instrument in creating a raging conspiracy to return her father to the throne by assassinating the current king, her grandfather Omer (see Ether 8:4–9). Along the way, she sees the death of a number of family members and, worse, the demise of her civilization. She begins the grisly journey by reminding her father, "Is there not an account concerning them of old, that they by their secret plans did obtain kingdoms and great glory?" (v. 9).

Secret combinations are nothing new to the Book of Mormon era. Cain can be considered the father of secret combinations, as he is the first to enter into a covenant with Satan (see Moses 5:38, 49), and the secret combination Jared's daughter adopts is traceable back to the original instigator through an evil system, "which had been handed down even from Cain, who was a murderer from the beginning" (Ether 8:15). These illicit covenants are so corrupt and dangerous that Moroni avoids revealing any details of "the manner of their oaths and combinations" (v. 20).

Yet Jared's daughter seems to be familiar, or at least able to educate herself, about the "record which our fathers brought . . . [explaining how] by their secret plans [they] did obtain kingdoms and great glory" (v. 9).

Jared's daughter coerces a man named Akish, a friend of her grandfather Omer, into desiring her as a wife when she dances for him.

The exchange for marriage is that Akish will bring the head of Omer to Jared. With this diabolical plan, many become caught up in Jared's daughter's conspiracy, including Akish's "kindred and friends" (v. 17). The plan moves forward with one deviation: the Lord warns Omer in a dream to flee the land in order to preserve his life.

In time, Akish marries the daughter of Jared, and Jared becomes king again. It seems the plan has worked, but all is not well. Jared's daughter has bargained for more than she could have ever conceived, and she soon discovers that no amount of prestige or wealth can make up for the evil she has introduced into her family. For in a subsequent scene, her husband, Akish, murders her father, effectively placing himself on the throne.

Akish's greed and distrust of others accelerates when he "[begins] to be jealous of his son" (Ether 9:7). This leads to a second devastating action. Akish starves his own son Shem in order to successfully remove at least one threat to the throne. This instigates a "war between the sons of Akish and Akish, which lasted for the space of many years, yea, unto the destruction of nearly all the people of the kingdom . . . save it were thirty souls" (v. 12).

And in the middle of all this turmoil? A woman who is a wife and now a grieving mother. What starts out as a plan to restore her father's kingdom ultimately results in a life of fear for Jared's daughter and the death of nearly all of her people, including her own son. It's no wonder Moroni blames the secret society she promotes as the downfall of the Jaredites and "the destruction of the people of Nephi" (Ether 8:21).

As with Isabel, the choices of this one woman affect the lives of many others—even an entire civilization—as her evil influence spreads far and wide. Satan is alive and well and can create terrible mischief through those who become his willing companions. We can all learn from the daughter of Jared's misdirected ambitions what paths *not* to follow. The daughter of Jared's choices illustrate how one woman can make a difference in many lives, for better or for worse, depending on the path she chooses.

Scriptures referencing the daughter of Jared: Ether 8:8–18.

Gomer, Wife of Hosea the Prophet

*So he went and took Gomer the daughter of Diblaim; which conceived,
and bare him a son.* (Hosea 1:3)

ALTHOUGH COMMENTATORS DEBATE WHETHER THE story of the
prophet Hosea's marriage to Gomer is figurative or literal, the
weight of the evidence in the story points to a real person named Gomer
and to her children, whom Hosea raises. And the story of her marriage,
as it is written, applies directly to the unfaithfulness of the Israelites to
the Lord during this era. It may also apply to unfaithfulness in our lives,
whether it be as serious as Gomer's indiscretions or more subtle, such as
not keeping all of our baptismal covenants.

Hosea's report affirms that he receives a command from the Lord to
marry "Gomer, the daughter of Diblaim." This may explain his devotion
to her as his wife—with a confirmation from the Lord about the spouse he
is to marry, it seems he is strengthened in his perseverance to stay married
to her. In time, she bears a son whom the Lord names "Jezreel" in
prophetic anticipation that "I [the Lord] will break the bow of Israel in the
valley of Jezreel" (Hosea 1:2–5). In this manner, the Lord involves Himself
in Gomer's life by giving her opportunity to escape her past as a former
harlot through an honorable marriage and by naming her first child.

Yet she makes choices that turn her life from good to bad. The
details are revealing. For the birth of Gomer's second child, a little girl,
Hosea writes that "she conceived again, and bare a daughter" (v. 6).
Unlike at the birth of her first child, wherein Hosea writes that Gomer
"bare him [Hosea] a son" (v. 3), the prophet omits mention of himself
as father for this second birth. Similarly, for Gomer's third child, a little
boy, we read simply that "she conceived, and bare a son" (v. 8). Again,
Hosea does not point to himself as father.

A last item fixes our view of Gomer. Over time, after she abandons Hosea, she becomes financially indebted to her current lover. Importantly, even after her ill behavior, the Lord does not give up on her, and her husband continues to love her, framing the two constants in her life. We hear the Lord's words directed at making her free: "Then said the Lord unto me [Hosea], Go yet, love a woman [Gomer] beloved of her friend, yet an adulteress, according to the love of the Lord toward the children of Israel. . . . So I bought her to me for fifteen pieces of silver, and for an homer of barley, and an half homer of barley," a huge price for her freedom (Hosea 3:1–3).

In one stroke, Hosea wipes away Gomer's financial debt. But she is forbidden to leave home for "many days," essentially putting her under house arrest (v. 3). How effective this house arrest is we do not learn. But in the category of lessons learned, we see that even though her infidelity mirrors the Israelites' infidelity with the Lord (see Hosea 2:2–3; 4:1–3), she enjoys the enduring love of her husband, and the Lord loves her too, just as He loves His people: "How shall I give thee up, Ephraim? how shall I deliver thee, Israel? . . . mine heart is turned within me, my repentings are kindled together. I will not execute the fierceness of mine anger . . . for I am God, and not man; the Holy One in the midst of thee" (Hosea 11:8–9).[51]

In our lives, there are times when we are given more than one chance to repent of the same mistake. Gomer's story emphasizes the opportunity each of us has to kneel before the Lord with a broken heart and contrite spirit and earn His forgiveness, not as a one-time event but as an ongoing purification.

The Savior's love is unconditional, just as Hosea's love for his wife remains unfettered. Our lives will be richer and our rise to our divine potential more sure as we humble ourselves and embrace the deliverance offered for our taking. Deliverance does not come cheaply, as the large amount Hosea paid for Gomer's release illustrates, but it comes with a fair and merciful price. And the price we pay will be worth the ultimate reward.

Scriptures referencing Gomer: Hosea 1; Hosea 3.

Section Five
Education of Ancient Women

EDUCATION AMONG ANCIENT WOMEN IS not necessarily found in reading and writing skills. In fact, it's a rare occurrence for a woman of ancient times to read or write. Education for these women comes in many other forms. Daughters learn cooking, weaving, childrearing, and housekeeping skills from their mothers, for the most part, and any formal education is reserved for sons, who are taught by skilled persons in their community, or by their fathers.

Some might claim Proverb 31:10–31 is an ancient-world handbook of sorts for young women who are preparing to marry in that era. Within these verses, we see guidance about virtue, righteousness, spinning and weaving, food preparation, planting, industry, serving the poor, taking care of clothing and appearance, and humility before the Lord. In the last verses, we see how they will receive their husband's and children's praise for following this guidance. Also added to this list is an interesting reference to education: "She openeth her mouth with wisdom; and in her tongue is the law of kindness" (v. 26). During this era, education does not take place in a formal setting such as a temple or school, in a business or workshop, but passes from woman to woman.

In Titus 2:3–5, we learn that it's the duty of the "aged women . . . [to be] teachers of good things" (v. 3). The older women teach the younger women to be sober, chaste, obedient, and faithful, and to love their husbands and children (see vv. 4–5). Upon further investigation, we discover that a handful of women did read and write. Jezebel writes letters "in Ahab's name, and sealed them with his seal" (1 Kings 21:8). King Ahasuerus asks Esther to "write ye also for the Jews . . . in the king's name" (Esther 8:8).

From the earliest of times, women are trained to fulfill certain roles, from that of a wife and mother to a queen. Esther's cousin Mordecai raises her after her own parents die. He educates and directs her, and even when she gains favor of the king, Esther looks to Mordecai in how to act: "For Esther did the commandment of Mordecai, like as when she was brought up with him" (Esther 2:20).

In the Book of Mormon, a woman has the political right to ascend to the Lamanite throne, as indicated in Alma 47:32–35. Amalickiah murders the king, then marries the queen to become king himself. Only through marrying the queen does Amalickiah gain royal power. This also demonstrates that the queen was educated and prepared enough to serve in this capacity, which may have included knowing more than one language. A few women throughout history are also known for speaking more than one language, as is the case with Queen Cleopatra VII, who was fluent in several languages.

In Proverb 8, wisdom is ascribed as a feminine characteristic (see vv. 1–3). On one level, the term seems to be answering the question, "With whom is God speaking when he mentions 'us' in Genesis 1:26?" On another, it clarifies the notion that *wisdom* is God's companion in creation.[52] This notion of wisdom as God's creation and then companion lies deep in scripture and associated literatures.[53]

In Solomon's case, the youthful king seeks wisdom as a constant companion, demonstrating the spiritual nature of education (see 1 Kings 4). The Book of Mormon is also connected with this stream of thought in Mosiah 8:20, where wisdom is portrayed as a feminine divine ruler—one the children of men do not "desire that she should rule over them!" In this connotation, wisdom is the blazer and keeper of the paths that mortals should walk in their lives (see Mosiah 2:36; Helaman 12:5). Moreover, she acts as an agent of God in accomplishing His will (see 2 Nephi 20:13, quoting Isaiah 10:13).

Other references to women as learners or teachers include the Song of Solomon: "Bring thee into my mother's house, who would instruct me" (8:2), the wise woman of Tekoa (see 2 Samuel 14:2–21), and the wise women of Abel (see 2 Samuel 20:16–22).

And finally, Jesus Christ is a champion of education for women, for He encourages Mary to sit at His feet and receive learning and instruction (see Luke 10:38–42). Christ clearly tells Martha that "Mary hath chosen that good part, which shall not be taken away from her" (v. 42).

Queen of Sheba

And when the queen of Sheba heard of the fame of Solomon concerning
the name of the Lord, she came to prove him with hard questions.
(1 Kings 10:1)

As IS CHARACTERISTIC OF ANCIENT societies, word about King
Solomon travels widely, aided by stunning news of his wisdom and
earthly abundance. In whichever country the Queen of Sheba lives—
Yemen, Oman, Ethiopia, or Egypt; there are cases made for all four—
she hears of Solomon. She's impressed with his wealth, but she also has
questions about matters of faith.

This all fulfills prophecy, adding ballast to the notion that the queen
is a spiritual woman. By seeking a more illuminating knowledge, the
Queen of Sheba satisfies part of her divine pining. A prophecy found
in Isaiah enlightens us that "all they from Sheba shall come: they shall
bring gold and incense; and they shall shew forth the praises of the
Lord" (Isaiah 60:6). The queen does both, giving Solomon "an hundred
and twenty talents of gold, and of spices great abundance" as well as
reason for praising his God for her inquisitive character (2 Chronicles
9:9).

It appears the queen already possesses a great deal of faith, which
she demonstrates when she speaks to Solomon. We are not privileged
to know what she says when she "commune[s] with him of all that
was in her heart" (v. 1), but we do know Solomon has answers to her
questions. This leads the queen to declare, "Thy [heavenly] wisdom and
[earthly] prosperity exceedeth the fame which I heard" (1 Kings 10:7).

Not surprisingly, the queen then takes opportunity to declare her own devotion to the Lord and bestow her royal blessing upon Solomon: "Blessed be the Lord thy God, which delighted in thee, to set thee on the throne of Israel: because the Lord loved Israel for ever, therefore made he thee king, to do judgment and justice" (1 Kings 10:9).

The queen's wisdom, augmented from Solomon and coupled with her faith in the Lord, allows her to become a faithful leader and, in the end, to "rise up in the judgment with the men of this generation, and condemn them" (Luke 11:31).

The Queen of Sheba is a strong leader and a woman with spiritual inclinations. When she hears of someone who possesses greater knowledge than she, the queen is willing to put forth a tremendous effort, as well as incur substantial cost, in order to educate herself, to improve herself. She has questions, and she determinedly seeks for answers.

How much stronger might we be in our little kingdoms—however small they may seem—if we seek answers from our wise and inspired prophets and leaders? In turn, like the Queen of Sheba, we'll gain additional wisdom and insight to govern our lives and to impart to those in our own spheres of influence.

Scriptures referencing the Queen of Sheba: 1 Kings 10:1–13; 2 Chronicles 9:1–12; Isaiah 60:6; Jeremiah 6:20.
Queen of the South: Matthew 12:42 and Luke 11:31.

Queen Esther

*And the king loved Esther above all the women, and she obtained grace
and favour in his sight more than all the virgins; so that he set the royal
crown upon her head, and made her queen instead of Vashti.*
(Esther 2:17)

FEW HISTORICAL WOMEN RISE FROM the status of commoner to sit
on a throne. That sort of story is almost always confined to legend
and mythology. But Esther, a lowly Jewish youth, succeeds.

The story of her rise to royalty begins when the king hosts a
week-long celebration for his courtiers in the palace. On the last day,
he orders his current queen, Vashti, to appear unveiled before the
assembled throng of men. True to her culture of feminine modesty,
she refuses. In his fury, the king puts Vashti under house arrest and
then accepts a suggestion that an empire-wide search be made for
a new queen (see Esther 1:10–2:4). Esther's cousin and guardian,
Mordecai, learns of this search and prepares Esther to become a
candidate (see Esther 2:8–10). Against all odds, she captures the fancy
of the king (see v. 17).

Besides her obvious beauty (see v. 7), Esther possesses other virtues,
not the least of which is a quick mind. Even though she likely grows
up not knowing how to read, she apparently learns after becoming
queen, for the royal decree ordering that all Jews be slain in the empire
is shown to her so she has visual proof of what it commands (see Esther
4:8).

Mordecai advises Esther to hide the fact that she is Jewish to
avoid having her heritage incur the king's wrath. But after five years

of marriage to King Ahasuerus, Esther faces an enormous challenge—that of saving her people from annihilation—in which she must reveal her true identity. Because she knows the written and unwritten rules of the palace, she uses them to her advantage when approaching this disclosure to her husband.

After the Jews in the capital city Shushan fast for three days for her mission, the critical moment arrives. She leaves her apartments for the throne room (see Esther 5:1). As she steps forward, she knows she may be walking to her death because without an invitation, no one is allowed to approach the king, including his wife (see Esther 4:11, 16). It is against palace law. Yet she also knows that if he extends his golden scepter to her, she is allowed to approach (see Esther 4:11, 16; 5:2). The crisis for her people looms so menacingly that she has to take action, even if it costs her life. With Mordecai's encouragement, Esther undertakes the almost impossible task of gaining the ear of the king. She takes Mordecai's counsel to heart when he says, "Think not with thyself" (Esther 4:13). Like many women, Esther puts the needs of her people and her family first.

Understanding the art of negotiation, Queen Esther does not ask for a favor at the first meeting or even the second (see Esther 5:4, 8). Instead, she waits until the third occasion, a lavish banquet, before voicing her request to the king (Esther 7:1–6). In each case, she shrewdly involves Haman, the man set on exterminating the Jews, in her meetings with the king. She is obviously not intimidated by this man who stands next to the throne, a position of enormous influence. Instead, she holds her ground and delivers her people, succeeding in her quest. Throughout the story, it becomes clear that Esther has been prepared both educationally and spiritually to come "to the kingdom for such a time as this" (Esther 4:14).[54]

Similar to Esther and other women throughout history, women in today's era are faced with many risks. Bearing children creates a physical risk. Women who stand up for their beliefs in the workplace take a financial risk. Women who follow the guidance of the Spirit take a risk of alienating themselves from what is popular in the world (see Esther 7:1–8:14).

We can learn from Esther's preparation for the momentous task of accomplishing the seemingly impossible. Her faithfulness and diligence in educating herself prove to be the characteristics that allow the Lord to work through her. As women today choose their paths of education and training and manage their study habits in both temporal and spiritual matters, they effectively open an avenue in which the Lord can use them as instruments in His hands. Instruments that may save an entire population, such as Queen Esther, or only one soul. Both are important in the Lord's eyes.

Scriptures referencing Esther: book of Esther.

Wives of Jared and His Brother

Go to and gather together thy flocks, both male and female, of every kind; and also of the seed of the earth of every kind; and thy families; and also Jared thy brother and his family; and also thy friends and their families, and the friends of Jared and their families. (Ether 1:41)

THE RESPONSIBILITIES OF FOUNDING A movement or a people of the Lord are often greater than those that fall on later generations. Even with divine help, the founders move forward into the unknown, needing skills and balance that come from both experience and training. In the cases of the wives of Jared and his brother, they form the glue that holds the moving camp together as they travel through uncharted terrestrial territories and twice cross major bodies of water.

Jared and the brother of Jared uproot their families and travel on two water journeys. The first is shorter, across an inland sea; the second requires sealed barges that can withstand the battering of deep ocean swells. The women of these families, particularly the wives, possess many skills they'll need to make adjustments in their new lands. Similar to other women who travel great distances as matriarchs among their people, the women of Jared's family face unending challenges in providing nourishment for their children and husbands.

The first part of their journey requires significant preparation before going into the valley of Nimrod (see Ether 2:1–3). The families work together to gather their flocks, capture fowls and fish with snares, then build vessels to transport them (see v. 2). They also collect swarms of bees and "seeds of every kind" (v. 3). These are all activities the women learn from each other, passing down the skills of how to survive in new and harsh lands.

When Jared's family and friends prepare for the journey, the Lord commands them to "travel in the wilderness, and . . . build barges" (v. 6). We don't know how much the women participate in the barge building, but we can assume they help in all tasks, working together as a community and employing their considerable skills.

After the families reach their new destination, the women are greeted with a different climate and new flora and fauna. Here, they must adjust whatever knowledge they have and find a way to provide for their families' welfare. They name the place where they set up camp on the seashore Moriancumer. When they reach this new land, the families live in tents for four years (see v. 13).

Tent construction and repair also falls to the women. Weaving tent panels would have taken a great deal of time, and the women have to keep up repairs because weather and climate tend to break down and batter even careful construction.[55]

The Lord sees fit to send Jared and the families to a new land yet again. They build new barges, this time with the tops sealed to protect them from the deep ocean. The Lord provides light by touching stones the brother of Jared brought Him. The women prepare "all manner of food, that they might subsist upon the water, and also food for their flocks and herds" (Ether 6:4).[56]

How the women deal with this new situation of floating beneath the high seas in such close confines day after day is difficult to comprehend. We learn that their barges are driven by a "furious wind," and that "they were tossed upon the waves of the sea" for 344 days (vv. 5, 11). Understandably, prayer becomes a regular part of the women's lives as they "cry unto the Lord" when the barges are submerged. Also, they "sing praises unto the Lord . . . and when the night came, they did not cease to praise the Lord" until they are delivered safely to land (vv. 7, 9).

It's no wonder that when the families touch ground again, "they bowed themselves down upon the face of the land . . . and . . . shed tears of joy" (v. 12). In their second location, much is to be done. Once again, the women have come to a new land with a new climate and a new set of circumstances. They "till the earth" (v. 13) and "begat sons and daughters" (v. 15), and "wax strong in the land" (v. 18)—the women have no small part as they work alongside the men. They demonstrate that a well-prepared woman makes an enormous difference in the welfare of her family members, whether in a familiar and comfortable situation or not.

This explains why the education and training of a woman continues to be so important today. We aren't required to select appropriate and edible plants in a foreign land or weave tent panels, but there are plenty of modern-life activities we must do. Education is more important than ever as some women need to support their families financially, as well as assist in the education of their children and others. Our world can be elevated to a better society when we put time and energy into our educations while still maintaining a relationship with God.

Scriptures referencing the wives indirectly:
Ether 1:33, 40–43; 2:1–7, 13; 6:3–4, 12–18.

Sariah, Wife of Lehi

And he came down by the borders near the shore of the Red Sea; and he traveled in the wilderness in the borders which are nearer the Red Sea; and he did travel in the wilderness with his family, which consisted of my mother, Sariah, and my elder brothers, who were Laman, Lemuel, and Sam. (1 Nephi 2:5)

DIVINE REVELATION AND SPIRITUAL REJUVENATION often flow to individuals in a challenging desert setting. For Sariah, wife of the prophet Lehi, a desert encampment somewhere in northwest Arabia becomes sacred to her because of an intensely inspiring experience she has there. In one defining moment, the Lord's Spirit rushes upon her and bears to her a testimony of her husband's calling and the Lord's power to deliver, specifically to deliver her sons (see 1 Nephi 5:7–8). In this remarkable sense, the Lord educates her.

Spiritual education is prime in the Lord's eyes. With our divinity moving along the right path, the Lord is able to bless us with other gifts, such as retention of information and recollection of thoughts and assurances. As we dedicate our education to the Lord, He blesses us in innumerable ways, which we see in Sariah's story.

Sariah becomes an anchoring foundation in the Lord's effort to bring her family and others safely to a land of promise and begin a new people of God, much as women today become anchors to their families. To this end, after the moment of the Lord's schooling her, Sariah bends all of her skills acquired over a lifetime to helping her traveling party traverse the desert and ocean successfully. Her participation in the exodus with her husband is essential to the survival of her family, both physically and spiritually. Little does she know that she is being prepared for a momentous undertaking, but the skills she learns as a girl and housewife in Jerusalem play an important role on the trail once her family sets foot on Arabian soil.

Like most women of her era, Sariah probably does not read and write. But she is an educated woman because she learns important life skills from her mother, and perhaps others, about plants and animals and their culinary characteristics. This knowledge, acquired as she grows to womanhood, becomes fundamental to the survival of her extended family in the desert. As the matriarch of the traveling band, she has charge of meals for almost twenty people.

To keep so many people alive in a harsh clime, with much of the vegetation and animal life unfamiliar to Sariah and with limitations on the meats she can prepare because of strictures in the Mosaic law requires deft ability and imagination. We know she possesses such skills because her group survives, even as it grows larger with the births of children (see 1 Nephi 17:1–2). To be sure, the traveling party carries "provisions" into the desert (1 Nephi 16:11), but they cannot pack enough on their animals to survive the long trek. Sariah learns to live off the inhospitable land, and that is where her abilities shine forth.

Once the family reaches Bountiful, a land of plenty, Sariah continues in her diligence and organization. She is the person to organize the "fruits and meat . . . and honey" that go aboard the ship for the long voyage to the New World, as well as a supply of fresh water (1 Nephi 18:6). Naturally, the travelers can take much more on the ship than they carry through the desert on the backs of pack animals. So the provisions are greater in amount (see v. 8), but the numbers in the traveling group have grown to perhaps more than forty persons. Hence, Sariah has to apportion foods and liquids judiciously so her family does not face starvation and thirst.

Honing skills such as preparing food seems a small thing, but when set against the backdrop of Sariah's experiences both in and out of the desert, it becomes the bread of life for her children. As she sets about her temporal and mundane tasks as matriarch, she is essentially giving her children nourishment so they might enjoy the greater blessings—that of coming unto the Lord. Sariah becomes an example to both men and women today as she scrapes together a living in a difficult situation and provides for her family through endurance and much faith.

Through the hard work and diligence of her hands, she nourishes and serves as the Savior serves: feeding her family and creating an atmosphere in which higher learning and true divinity can be achieved. Thus, Sariah's skills and abilities turn the key for the Lord to bring her people safely and healthily to the promised land.[57]

In our lives, we experience challenges similar to Sariah's in which we need to be more creative in preparing meals or providing clothing and other necessities for our children when our budget is tight. We aren't asked to go on an eight-year camping trip like Sariah, but we endure another sort of wilderness trek: determining to live within our means, living frugally even when finances are healthy, will go a long way when we hit financial hardships.

Scriptures referencing Sariah: 1 Nephi 1:1; 2:5; 5:1–8; 8:14–16; 17:1–2; 18:17–18.

Conclusion
Our Divine Nature

To rise to the divine within us is to become like our Savior: full of charity, understanding, and experience. Every person born on earth arrives with inherent divinity, but we must each cultivate and strive to fill our lives with things divine in order to achieve exaltation. Opening our hearts to the Lord's teachings and His will enables us to retain our divinity and walk the path that leads to our eternal reward.

When our last day on earth passes into the shadow of the approaching twilight, each woman's name may not be heralded far and wide in a worldly sense, but each has the opportunity to be numbered among the nobility of heaven.

By studying women who have gone before us and how, with heaven's help, they have handled their various callings and duties, both small and lofty, women find strength and comfort in the fact that they are not alone in their duties and responsibility of making correct choices. As we all know, choices that may seem insignificant today do have eternal importance. In reality, a woman's daily tasks and decisions create the warp and weft of her soul and the souls of those she influences. Importantly, she must resist the allure of the messages the world sends to her, that status and power really matter. These messages are not what we learn from our Savior. As the nature of divinity slowly weaves itself together in her being, through faith and endurance a woman will come to understand just how noble and precious her heritage is and how she can embrace the divine roles with which she has been entrusted.

In order to identify more clearly the paths we must take to achieve the highest honor of exaltation, we can look to women of the past who have faced similar choices, such as Mother Eve. Scores of scholarly papers, as well as scriptural accounts and works of fiction, have been written about Eve, the first mortal woman on earth, and they generally converge into one idea: she is a courageous woman who, despite heart-wrenching trials, lives a righteous life and remains true to her covenants. That is the epitome of the life of a divine woman and defines divine nature as one who faces the winds of trials pushing her in all directions and remains steadfast in her covenants to the Lord.

Because Eve and Adam empowered the process of procreation and childbirth, our spirits can come to earth to fulfill our own divine missions. Although specific callings on earth may vary from woman to woman, each is given the choice to embrace her divine callings or welcome the accolades and tempting voices of the world. Just as Eve faced choices, some inspired by the devil himself, so do all women. The question becomes, which choice will each woman make? Throughout this book, we've examined woman's divine heritage and eternal nature from the viewpoint of women who lived during ancient times. How they embrace opportunities and make their choices varies, yet their examples are sources of instruction.

In our modern-day lives filled with numerous challenges, some women may question their divine role. They may compare their lives to those around them and wonder why they receive such a meager allotment of blessings when it seems others are flourishing. Some see other women with seemingly perfect families, their children lined up in the chapel pew, arms folded over their pressed clothing while their own family enjoys no such order or peace. Others witness women who are able to balance family life and careers with apparent ease as they themselves struggle to make even one of those work for their family.

In another vein, one woman finds herself as the eternal primary teacher, handing out tissues for runny noses, asking little girls to keep their dresses down and little boys to stop elbowing each other. Another woman experiences rejection in the workplace, seemingly destined to always be looking for meaningful employment. Some face serious challenges with their children or other family members, whether they are physical or psychological or spiritual. Still others find themselves struggling to make ends meet at key moments in life or to keep themselves physically and emotionally fit.

History is filled with accounts of women who have overcome seemingly insurmountable odds and still accomplish great deeds. We've discussed a number of them in the ancient scriptural texts—including prophetesses, priestesses, queens, wives of prophets, and daughters of kings. Even though most women never obtain any such title on earth, women everywhere today enjoy laudable personal victories as these ancient women did. To the point, modern women have a calling that supersedes any who's who list and tops every worldly accolade: they are divine women. They are noble daughters of God.

As we've discussed women of the Old Testament, New Testament, and Book of Mormon, and how these women fulfilled their divine callings, we see how womanhood is a calling in itself. Women are the inheritors of Mother Eve's remarkable traits. And callings and opportunities come in the form of achieving education, leading people, prophesying, interpreting visions and revelations, or discovering the consequences of straying from the path. The acceptance of the divinity within each of us lifts us above our hardships and mortal labors. Specifically, a woman's divine calling, carefully nurtured and cultivated, offers a sense of inner serenity and enduring value. With this knowledge, her divinity will shape her soul and aid her in conquering any trial standing in her path.

About the Authors

Heather B. Moore is the two-time Best of State and two-time Whitney Award winner for her historical fiction, the most recent release being *Esther the Queen.* She is also the author of the nonfiction inspirational book *Women of the Book of Mormon* and the coauthor of *Christ's Gifts to Women* with Angela Eschler. Heather is a columnist for *Meridian Magazine* on LDS topics.

Dr. S. Kent Brown is the author of scores of doctrinal works and scripture commentaries, and he is the executive producer of the *Messiah* film series. His educational background includes a PhD in religious studies, and he has served as the chair of Ancient Scripture at BYU, the director of the BYU-Jerusalem Center, editor in chief of the *Journal of Book of Mormon Studies,* and associate director of the Neal A. Maxwell Institute. He currently serves as the New Testament scholar consultant for the LDS.org film vignettes on the Savior's life.

In Appreciation

MANY THANKS TO OUR ADVANCE readers who offered invaluable insight and advice: Lu Ann Staheli, Debra Erfert, Estee Wood, Annette Lyon, and Gayle Brown.

Endnotes

1 http://www.lds.org/topics/family-proclamation

2 See M. Russell Ballard, "Learning the Lessons of the Past," *Ensign*, May 2009.

3 See Bible Dictionary, s.v. "Revelation," and D&C 28:2–8; 100:11; 107:91–92.

4 Through her husband's visions and visitations, Sarah receives her own personal instruction about how to live her life and how to save her husband's life. While Abraham and Sarah are traveling into Egypt, the Lord tells Abraham that Sarah must act as if she is his sister instead of his wife: "When the Egyptians shall see her, they will say—She is his wife, and they will kill you, but they will save her alive" (Abraham 2:23). They do this so the Egyptian men will think they have a chance with the "fair" Sarah; whereas if she were married, they would kill her husband in order to free her (v. 22).

5 It's important to note that Abraham does not take a handmaiden of his own volition; he makes no move concerning his seed until Sarah bids him to: "Abram hearkened unto the voice of Sarai" (Genesis 16:2). The decision for the prophet to take a handmaiden is Sarah's choice, referred to as "the law of Sarah" (D&C 132:65).

6 See *Old Testament Student Manual: Genesis—2 Samuel*, 76–77; and JST, Genesis 22:7; and Louis Ginzberg in *The Legends of the Jews*, trans. Henrietta Szold (Philadelphia: The Jewish Publication of America, 1937), 1:275–276.

7 See "Turn to the Lord" by Elder Donald H. Hallstrom, in which he counsels Church members to turn to the Lord in our times of trial to let Him share our burdens (*Ensign*, May 2010, 78–80).

8 Samson's mother remains unnamed, and only her husband Manoah receives a name in the scriptural account. But in accord with an old pattern, she will receive a name among neighbors as soon as her newborn arrives: "Mother of Samson"—just as Noah's wife's name becomes "mother of Japheth" after giving birth to her firstborn (Moses 8:12).

9 Sources for "Mother of Samson" segment: J. Cheryl Exum, "Manoah," in *The Anchor Bible Dictionary*, ed. David Noel Freedman et al., 6 volumes (New York: Doubleday, 1992), 4:511–12; Donald W. Parry and Stephen D. Ricks, "The Judges of Israel (Judges)," *Studies in Scripture, Volume Three: Genesis to 2 Samuel*, ed. Kent P. Jackson and Robert L. Millet (Salt Lake City, UT: Randall Book Co., 1985), 239–47.

10 Source for "Rebekah" segment: Bruce R. McConkie, "The Promises Made to the Fathers," *Studies in Scripture, Volume Three:Genesis to 2 Samuel*, ed. Kent P. Jackson and Robert L. Millet (Salt Lake City, UT: Randall Book Co., 1985), 58–59.

11 John L. Sorenson, *Images of Ancient America: Visualizing the Book of Mormon* (Provo, Utah: FARMS, 1998), 156. Additional scriptures on bodies left unburied: Alma 2:37–38; 16:10–11.

12 See Miriam Feinberg Vamosh, *Women at the Time of the Bible* (Herzlia, Israel: Palphot Ltd., 2007), 55.

13 Simon Peter and the Lord's brother James are the other two, in addition to Mary, who see the resurrected Lord (see Luke 24:34; John 20:1–2, 11–18; 1 Corinthians 15:5, 7).

14 Sources for "Women of Galilee" segment: Joel B. Green, *The Gospel of Luke, The New International Commentary on the New Testament* (Grand Rapids, MI: Eerdmans, 1997), 316–21, 850–60.
Leon Morris, *Luke: An Introduction and Commentary*, rev. ed. (Grand Rapids, MI: Eerdmans, 1988), 164–65, 362–65.

15 Sources for "Lydia" segment: Frederick Fyvie Bruce, *Paul: The Apostle of the Heart Set Free* (Grand Rapids, MI: Eerdmans, 1977), 219–22; Holland L. Hendrix, "Philippi," in *The Anchor Bible Dictionary*, 5:313–17.

Jerome Murphy-O'Connor, *Paul: A Critical Life* (Oxford: Clarendon Press, 1996), 211–15.

Ben Witherington, III, "Lydia (Person)," in *The Anchor Bible Dictionary*, 4:422–23.

16 Sources for the "Mary" segment: *Mishnah Hagigah* 1.1, trans. Herbert Danby (London: Oxford University Press, 1972); Frederick Fyvie Bruce, *The Acts of the Apostles: The Greek Text with Introduction and Commentary* (Grand Rapids, MI: Eerdmans, 1951), 74; Joseph A. Fitzmyer, "The Gospel According to Luke," *The Anchor Bible*, 2 vols. (New York: Doubleday, 1981, 1885), 1:440.

17 Sources for the "Widow at the Temple" segment: Mishnah, *Shekalim* 6.5; Leon Morris, *Luke: An Introduction and Commentary*, rev. ed. (Grand Rapids, MI.: Eerdmans, 1988), 321–22.

18 Sources for the "Woman with the Issue of Blood" segment: Joel B. Green, *The Gospel of Luke*, The New International Commentary on the New Testament (Grand Rapids, MI: Eerdmans, 1997), 346–49.
Leon Morris, *Luke: An Introduction and Commentary*, rev. ed. (Grand Rapids, MI: Eerdmans, 1988), 174–76.

19 Beverly Campbell, *Eve and the Choice Made in Eden* (Salt Lake City, UT: Bookcraft, 2003), 53.

20 Richard D. Draper, S. Kent Brown, Michael D. Rhodes, *The Pearl of Great Price: A Verse-by-Verse Commentary* (Salt Lake City, UT: Deseret Book Company, 2005), 235.

21 Robert J. Matthews, "Fall of Adam," The Neal A. Maxwell Institute, http://maxwellinstitute.byu.edu/publications/books/?bookid=51&chapid=370

22 Campbell, *Eve and the Choice Made in Eden,* 14.

23 Draper et al., *The Pearl of Great Price: A Verse-by-Verse Commentary*, 43.

24 Hannah's song of thanksgiving might be compared to Mary's psalm of praise when she meets with her cousin Elisabeth—both women with child (see Luke 1:46–55).

25 Routine sacrifices throughout Mesoamerica included blood sacrifices, such as animal and human blood (autosacrificing or removing the head or heart). The priests made these sacrifices in behalf of an individual or community. The smoke that rose from a sacrifice was believed to be sweet to the "nostrils of the gods" (*Images of Ancient America*, 142). Autosacrificing was a form of bloodletting, or giving back life to the gods who created the sky and earth (Michael D. Coe, *The Maya, Seventh Edition*. New York: Thames & Hudson, 2005,13). John L. Sorenson has suggested that human sacrifice may be part of the "abominations" Nephi prophesied of in 1 Nephi 12:23 (*Images*, 142).

26 Hugh Nibley, *Teachings of the Book of Mormon—Part Two* (Provo, Utah: FARMS, 2004), 309.

27 In *Old Testament Student Manual: Genesis–2 Samuel*, 254.

28 Vamosh, 53.

29 Wet nurses are employed by wealthy women and, more specifically in this case, by women who haven't given birth to an adopted child (see Vamosh, 51).

30 Josephus refers to the scene where Miriam suggests that a Hebrew woman become Moses's nurse in *Antiquities*, vol. 4 (Cambridge, MA: Harvard University Press), 2.9.5, no. 226.

31 See Vamosh, 67.

32 See Vamosh, 88

33 Vamosh, 87.

34 The First Temple, also known as Solomon's Temple, was constructed in the tenth century BC and was later destroyed in 587 BC.

35 See Vamosh, 91.

36 See Vamosh, 87.

37 See Leviticus 12:2–5: For a male child, the woman is unclean for seven days, and the days of purification last thirty-three days; for a female child, the woman is unclean fourteen days, and purification lasts sixty-six days.

38 Sources for "Isaiah's Wife" segment: Keith A. Meservy, "God Is with Us (Isaiah 1–17)," in *Studies in Scripture, Volume Four: 1 Kings to Malachi*, Kent P. Jackson, ed. (Salt Lake City, UT: Deseret Book, 1993), 95–98; Sidney B. Sperry, *The Voice of Israel's Prophets* (Salt Lake City, UT: Deseret Book, 1952), 28–30.

39 See "Nehemiah: Builder of Walls and Wills," *Old Testament Student Manual: 1 Kings—Malachi*, 335.

40 Sources for "Elisabeth" segment: S. Kent Brown, *Mary and Elisabeth: Noble Daughters of God* (American Fork, Utah: Covenant Communications, 2002), 21–33; S. Kent Brown, "Zacharias and Elisabeth, Joseph and Mary," in *The Life and Teachings of Jesus Christ: From Bethlehem through the Sermon on the Mount*, ed. Richard Neitzel Holzapfel and Thomas A. Wayment (Salt Lake City, UT: Deseret Book, 2005), 91–120.

41 Sources for "Daughters of Philip" segment: Frederick Fyvie Bruce, *The Acts of the Apostles: The Greek Text with Introduction and Commentary* (Grand Rapids, MI: Eerdmans, 1951), 386–87; Bruce R. McConkie, *Doctrinal New Testament Commentary* (Salt Lake City, UT: Bookcraft, 1970), 2:180–81.

42 Robert Matthews cites more scriptural examples of false worship and religious cults in his article "What the Scriptures Say about Astrology, Divination, Spirit Mediums, Magic, Wizardy, and Necromancy," *Ensign*, March 1974,

43 "Chapter 13: Stand by the Truth Lest You Be Deceived," *Teachings of Presidents of the Church: Joseph F. Smith*, 117.

44 Ibid., 118.

45 See Vamosh, 58.

46 For a summary of divination practices, see Matthews, *Ensign*, March 1974,

47 See Bible Dictionary, s.v. "Jezebel."

48 See Nibley, *Teachings of the Book of Mormon*, 371.

49 See *Old Testament Student Manual, 1 Kings—Malachi*, 235–37.

50 King Jared II was born several generations after the original Jared who crossed the ocean. The genealogy of Jared is outlined in Dennis L. Largey, *Book of Mormon Reference Companion* (Salt Lake City, UT: Deseret Book, 2003), s.v. "Jared."

51 Sources for "Gomer" segment: S. Kent Brown, "The Book of Hosea," *Studies in Scripture: Volume Four, 1 Kings to Malachi*, ed. Kent P. Jackson (Salt Lake City, UT: Deseret Book, 1993), 61–67; Abraham J. Heschel, *The Prophets* (Philadelphia, PA: Jewish Publication Society of America, 1962), 50–57; Harold H. Rowley, "The Marriage of Hosea," *Bulletin of the John Rylands Library* 39 (1956–57): 200ff; Sidney B. Sperry, *The Voice of Israel's Prophets* (Salt Lake City, UT: Deseret Book, 1965), 279–84.

52 In Proverb 8:22–36, Wisdom appears from the beginning as a heavenly created personality who participates in the Creation and then aids in setting bounds and limits both to the earth itself and to God's children. See the comments of John Marsh, *St John*, 97, 99–100, 103.

53 This notion is closely mirrored in *Wisdom of Ben Sira* (or *Sirach*) 1:4–10, a work in the Old Testament Apocrypha. Her description in the *Wisdom of Solomon* 7:22–8:1, in the same collection, is closer to the attributes ascribed to the *Logos*, or Word, in John 1. Herbert G. May and Bruce Metzger, eds., *The New Oxford Annotated Bible with the Apocrypha* (New York: Oxford University Press, 1977).

54 Sources for "Esther" segment: David J. A. Clines, "Mordecai (Person)," in *The Anchor Bible Dictionary*, 4:902–3; Roland Kenneth Harrison, *Introduction to the Old Testament* (Grand Rapids, MI: Eerdmans, 1969),

1085–1102; Carey A. Moore, "Esther, Book of," in *The Anchor Bible Dictionary*, 2:633–34.

55 Charles Doughty explains that the nomadic lifestyle for ancient women throughout Arabia was full of responsibilities, i.e., the setting up of tents, taking them down, loading supplies onto camels, preparing meals, making clothing, guarding flocks, gathering firewood, churning butter, and collecting water. *Travels in Arabia Deserta*, 2 vols. (New York: Random House, 1936), 1:262.

56 Ibid.

57 Sources for "Sariah" segment: Susan Easton Black, "Sariah," in *Book of Mormon Reference Companion*, ed. Dennis L. Largey et al. (Salt Lake City, UT: Deseret Book, 2003), 701; Camille Fronk, "Desert Epiphany: Sariah and the Women in 1 Nephi," in *Journal of Book of Mormon Studies* vol. 9, no. 2 (Provo, UT: FARMS, 2000), 4–15; George D. Potter, "A New Candidate for the 'Valley of Lemuel,'" *Journal of Book of Mormon Studies*, vol. 8, no. 1 (Provo, UT: FARMS, 1999), 54–63; John L. Sorenson, "The Composition of Lehi's Family," in *By Study and Also by Faith: Essays in Honor of Hugh Nibley*, 2 vols., ed. John M. Lundquist and Stephen D. Ricks (Salt Lake City, UT: Deseret Book, 1990), 2:174–96.

Art Credits

Page viii: *Blessed Art Thou* © 2013 Howard Lyon – For print information go to www.fineart.howardlyon.com or call 480-241-7907.

Page xii: *Is Anything Too Hard For The Lord* © 2013 by Elspeth Young. All Rights Reserved. May not be copied.

Page 18: *For This Child I Prayed* © 2013 by Elspeth Young. All Rights Reserved. May not be copied.

Page 44: *The Substance Of Hope* © 2013 by Elspeth Young. All Rights Reserved. May not be copied.

Page 74: *Waiting For The Promise* © 2013 by Elspeth Young. All Rights Reserved. May not be copied.

Page 90: *The Promised Land* © 2013 by Elspeth Young. All Rights Reserved. May not be copied.

Page 108: *First Blossom* © 2013 by Annie Henry. Courtesy of Altus Fine Art. For print information, visit www.altusfineart.com.